Oh, by the way...

a wonderful way to sell and be sold to

Brian Buffini

olivemount™
press
Carlsbad, CA 92009

Oh, by the way... ™

1st edition
1 December 2002

Printed in the U.S.A.

Dedication

to

Bev and the A Team,
my Mother and Father,
the People of Providence

Contents

Introduction

People have asked me many times about the secrets to success. I always refer to the persons I've associated with and the books I've read. Having recommended many books over the years, I decided to write one myself.

It's a long way from the streets of Dublin to Carlsbad, California, and I'd like to relate my joyful journey to you in these pages. I started out as a housepainter's son, came to America, and became a realtor®. After much trial and error, I developed a wonderful system for doing business. It made my business a success and changed my life for the better. Then, one day, my bride Beverly changed my life even more dramatically. "The system has improved our lives so much and we meet so many people who are struggling," she said to me, "that you need to go out and share it with others." Now, it's not usually a good thing when your wife tells you to hit the road, but in this instance it turned out to be providential.

I began teaching the system to people and found out that it was not only transferable, but transformational. What started out as a project to help people has turned into the largest coaching company in America. Over 600,000 have attended our seminars. I put my system and ideas in print to give more people the opportunity to experience a turning point in their business and life. Enjoy the book.

CHAPTER 1

Starting and learning the hard way

When I arrived in San Diego from Dublin, I was filled with excitement and the anticipation that only an immigrant can feel. While I was excited about being in America and its opportunities, I was terrified because I had hardly any money and virtually nothing to fall back on. Mom and Dad had remained in Ireland. They didn't have the money to support my adventurous spirit, and I was on my own. Given all that, failure was a consideration, but not an option. I had to make it here in America.

So I came to the city of opportunity...San Diego...in the golden state of California...a paradise of perfect weather, beautiful beaches, and suntanned, successful people. And I, seeking success, had no idea what I wanted to do or how I'd make my living. I had no plan because back then I hadn't yet realized the great value of long-term thinking.

Unknowing, untanned and unprepared, I took the common, conventional approach. I surveyed the job market, found my way around, and read the classified ads. I remember on the first Sunday I arrived there was an ad in the San Diego newspaper for a Sales & Marketing Executive at a salary of $70,000, which was pretty high compensation at that time. It seemed to me a fortune. I answered the ad and finagled an interview. And I had to take a bus to get there. It took about forty minutes on the bus to get to that important interview.

If you'd seen me in my job interview get-up, you'd have been on the floor laughing. Imagine a clueless kid, just come over from Ireland, in a white shirt, leather jacket and thin leather tie. What did I know of style and business suits and what to wear to a high-powered Sales & Marketing interview? My costume was all the rage in Europe; I didn't realize it was not high style in California. That was only one of many things I didn't realize. I had a lot to learn in this New World.

When I arrived at the office for my interview, they asked me to sit down and fill out a whole bunch of paperwork. Keep in mind that I'd only been in this country for a couple of days. There were questions on the forms like:

"What is my drivers license number?" I didn't have one.

"What's my social security number?" Didn't have one.

"What's your address?" Couldn't remember.

When I completed the application, I had only filled out about two of the twenty lines. The one thing I could properly answer was where I was from; the form asked *Place of Birth*, and I wrote "Dublin". When the lady called me forward, she asked, "Is that Dublin, Ohio, Mr. Buffini?", and I knew I was in trouble. This whole thing wouldn't fly. No social security number, no drivers license; I had to get all that; and they thought Dublin was in Ohio! Officially, I didn't exist! Here I was applying for a Sales & Marketing Executive position, and I couldn't even fill out the application because I lacked the essentials of American identification.

So I moved around and took whatever jobs I could get. I sold T-shirts down at the beach and engaged in a wide variety of similar executive tasks to make a modest living. Through it all, I knew I wanted a solid job in sales. I enjoyed people and thought sales would be a fine career.

They say that a bar is an Irishman's office, and it proved true for me. One day, after I'd been here a bit, I happened to meet a salesman named Bill Johnson. We were sitting next to each other at the bar in a restaurant and simply began having a great chat. He asked me about Ireland, and I asked him about San Diego. During the course of the conversation, I asked Bill what he did for a living. He replied that he was a real estate salesman. That sounded right up my alley, so I started asking him all about it. What did he do? How did he do it? What did it take to do it?

He was more than happy to tell me all about his real estate career...very enthusiastically.

And he handed me his business card. Well, I had never seen a business card like this before. First thing I noticed in the top right corner was a full-color picture of him. The photograph looked so good that I did several double-takes because it didn't look anything like the man sitting next to me. He assured me it was himself.

Next, down on the bottom left corner of this business card was a gold star. Inside the gold star were the words *Million Dollar Club*. Well, you can imagine my reaction. There I was, a fifth-generation painter and decorator's son from the south side of Dublin, Ireland...not Ohio; I grew up in an average neighborhood in a financially dis-advantaged country at that time. This was the first time in my life that I had come in contact with a real live gen-uine millionaire. I was blown away, tremendously excited to be hobnobbing with this hugely successful person!

I asked Bill about the Million Dollar Club. It all seemed to go together. He wore an expensive suit, drove a fancy car, and certainly gave the signals that he was success-ful. I later found out that the Million Dollar Club means the agent sold a million dollars worth of real estate, which represents $30,000 in commissions for the year. His broker probably got half, so that meant he made $15,000. He probably paid about $5,000 just to be in the business, so his total earnings from a million dollars in sales were probably about $10,000. The poverty line in the United States in the mid-80s was about $16,400. But

I didn't realize then that the man I thought was a millionaire, who had *Million Dollar Club* on his business card, was actually below the poverty line, hardly making a living. And I have come to learn that such can be the nature of sales.

A few days later, I visited Bill at his office. He gave me a tour, and I met his fellow agents and his broker. Every time I was introduced, each agent handed me a business card, and every card had this little Million Dollar Club symbol on it. Keep in mind that I believed they were all millionaires. I thought it was wonderful; that the streets were truly lined with gold in California; that I had lucked out and landed in a place where millionaires are quickly made, like cookies. Well, if everyone was a millionaire, I was pretty sure I could become one, too!

To give you an idea of my excitement and anticipation right then, I was like a shaken can of soda...ready to explode. However, I contained myself, approached the broker and asked what I had to do to get into this real estate business. She sketched it out for me, told me how to go about getting a license, and invited me back for an interview...after I passed the licensing exam.

I enrolled directly in a real estate school and started studying earnestly for the exam. After several months of primarily pounding through paperwork, I got my license, not a remarkably difficult exercise in itself.

After a month or two of continued study and odd jobs to generate some income, I started my real estate career. I remember my very first day on the job, walking in the door with absolutely no concept of what I was supposed to be doing. I had no idea how real estate worked, how leads came in, how you actually made sales. However, I was dressed superbly for business American-style; I had learned the perceptive difference between a business outfit and a leather jacket. I walked in the door, and the broker showed me to my designated desk. This was a big deal to me because everyone in our family had always been tradesmen. Now here I was, the fifth-generation painter's son, coming to work in an office with a desk of my own. And I was wearing a shirt and tie. The shirt was white and the tie was silk, not leather. I was now officially a white-collar worker, as we'd say back home.

> Not only does Brian tenaciously overcome challenges, he systemizes the solutions so those challenges never occur again.
> — John Buffini

There I was...totally fired up, ready to go, just needing to be pointed in the right direction. Young, eager, clueless. I was about to have the wind taken out of my sales.

First thing, the broker handed me a big, fat book. She told me it was an important tool of the trade. It was called *a crisscross directory*, a listing of all home-owners on the streets in the neighborhoods in the vicinity of the office. Basically, it's a phone book tied to street addresses.

The next thing she gave me was a one-page script detailing how to get on the phone and call all the people in the book to ask them if they're interested in selling their home. We role-played, using the script, to familiarize me with the procedure. She'd pretend to be a seller and I'd pretend to be an agent. At that time, I was definitely pretending to be an agent! We practiced back and forth and switched roles. She showed me how an expert does it, and after an hour of practicing she decided I'd gotten the gist of it.

"Okay, Brian, are you ready to make some calls?"
"Sure!" I replied with utmost confidence. I was ready.

As I made my first call, she gave me some last-minute advice: "Brian, there are just two things you need to remember. Number one, in this office our policy is that you call until you get an appointment. It might take you a half hour. It might take you an hour. It might take all day. It doesn't matter. That's it. You just stay on that phone until you get an appointment. Number two, don't worry about it. These people will love talking to you. Now just go ahead and start calling."

So I punched the numbers on the phone, and, in my most cultivated south Dublin accent, I very politely inquired,

"Hello, my name is Brian Buffini. I was wondering if you might be interested in selling your home."

There was a short interval of heavy breathing, then the response came back loudly in my right ear, "I don't need any frickin' realtors calling me at home. Get lost! Drop dead!" Bang! The phone was hung up with force to match the words.

To say I was a little taken aback would be an understatement. I'd come from a culture that was very hospitable. I'd never experienced cold-calling at home in Ireland. Back there, no one had ever cold-called my house. Most of my neighbors didn't even have telephones. Maybe it was just a one-time experience, just one bad apple. I had to get past this troubling reaction to my very first attempt at real estate sales. So I tried again. And again. And again.

That entire first day, I stayed on the phone calling unreceptive home-owners. For seven hours I did what the broker had directed me to do. After a full day of rejection, I came to the realization that these people did not love talking to me. In fact, most, if not all, were extraordinarily ticked off to hear from me. Yes, you get to wear a white shirt every day, but this is also what you get in the normal world of sales.

At that moment, I came to the conclusion that I didn't want to do this for the rest of my life. I stomped into the broker's office, put the book down on her desk, and declared, "You know what, I'm not going to do this again. Do you have anything else I can do around here?"

She described other sales techniques favored for use by the agency. One of these Million Dollar Club methods was the *expired listing* . An expired listing is a home that doesn't sell after being on the market for six months. These show up on the Multiple Listing Service so that real estate agents know which homes haven't sold and are now fair game. The morning after listings expire, every agent in the county calls the home-owners to request the re-listing. Again, it's a process of pounding people on the telephone.

The broker showed me the dialogue for the expired listings approach. I thought this technique made sense, since people who want to sell their homes should be happy to hear from a realtor. I was not aware that, on the same morning I would be calling them, there had been other agents calling since 7:00 AM. By noon, the poor home-owner had probably received twenty or thirty re-listing calls. After diligently preparing and practicing, it was about noon when I got around to placing my calls. These home-owners were not only unhappy to hear from me, they were royally pissed off. They screamed at me on the phone and gave me hell for bothering them. I stayed with it, and it went on like that all day.

Now I'm realizing this isn't exactly what I thought it would be. In fact, my dad's painting and decorating profession looked better and better with each call I made. But there I was, an immigrant wanting to be successful, determined to make a go of it...willing to get back on the phone to do whatever it took to make some sales...but not willing to be cursed at.

The broker shared her next sales technique with me: "What you can do, Brian, is go door to door, asking people if they want to sell their home."

I tried that, but as I walked around, knocking on people's doors asking them to sell their home, I felt like an idiot. It didn't produce much, but I did it. And I did get into some engaging conversations with some nice folks. Some of the older ones were just happy to have somebody stop by and talk to them for a while. It soon became apparent that this method was neither productive nor my cup of tea.

The final proven sales method recommended to me by the broker was contacting *For-Sale-By-Owners*, known as *FSBOs*. These were people who were selling their homes themselves. Many had signs in their yards that warned: "No real estate agents" or "Don't call" or "Do not bother owner." I liked the challenge of trying to get in the door, but I found it meant dealing with some unpleasant people. They were largely distrustful of agents and suspicious of my motivations. They knew I wanted to make the sale, but not that I also genuinely wanted to do a good job on their behalf. That didn't translate for them. Almost all questioned my integrity and my intentions. I actually did convert a number of these for-sale-by-owners to listings for myself. Even though I made some commissions this way, it was not totally satisfying. But at least and at last, I had something going.

I also had something going on inside me...a severe problem with these traditional sales approaches. They all created conflicts of conscience within me. I needed sales and income, but I had a hard time doing to others what I didn't want done to me. I've always resisted having others impose their will on me. Now I was being urged to impose my will on others, to pound people until they made a decision, whether they wanted to or not, whether they knew me or liked me or trusted me.

I didn't like the idea of people calling me at home at night, but now I was calling other people at home at night. It's odd how following the established practices of a business can bring you to do things against your nature.

While I was knocking on doors, I started thinking about the funny contrariness of it. Back home in Ireland, we'd be visited by a door-to-door salesperson only occasionally. Whenever someone came down our street knocking on doors, my mother ran around our house hollering at the top of her voice, "Get down, get down! Don't open that door!" You'd have thought it was the Mafia knocking. Now, years later and in a different culture, I find myself knocking on doors for a living. It turns out I'm the bogeyman on the outside while moms shout at their kids to stay down and not answer the door. The bad guy at your door was not a role I was going to play long-term.

I started searching for alternatives. There had to be other ways to make sales in real estate. There had to be ways that were not offensive, that actually appealed to people and served them well, that I would welcome if I were in their place...and I'd find them.

In all forms of sales, there are walk-ins. These are people who come to a sales office seeking service. They actually walk in or call. In the real estate business, waiting for them is called *floor time*. An assigned agent sits in the office to take incoming phone calls for the company. It offers the agent the opportunity to connect with any stray lead or anyone looking for information. It also gives the agent the chance to capture a client. While it is a valid way to generate leads, it is totally passive.

During my beginnings in business, I spent many days doing floor time, answering the office phone without talking to a single lead. It struck me as a form of "doing time." I'd bring a box of cookies, spend the entire day by myself, and eat all of the cookies. It was a very slow way to do business. But many agents still waste their time with it, just sitting around waiting for people to call.

Another passive system is the Open House. The agent sits in the designated house all day and hopes that people will come...with no guarantee that anyone will show up. Spend four or five hours on a Saturday or Sunday afternoon just hoping someone walks in. Even if someone comes, they're not necessarily going to buy. Or they're probably connected to another agent. Or they're just sport-lookers wanting to see the inside of someone else's home. In any case, the Open House is not a very productive way to generate sales or leads.

I was directed to all of these traditional sales methods, tried them all, found them wanting, and registered my dissatisfaction with all of them. It seemed to me that dependence on traditional selling methods gave a false feeling of control. That's because you go with the flow and know that at least minimal leads will eventually come of using the old methods. You feel secure in selling the same way that everyone else does. And if traditional ways don't work for you, you have their failure in common with everyone else. That's wonderfully self-excusing, but not productive or effective. I saw two major problems with the traditional methods: first, they proved expensive ways to generate a lead; second, the leads were not usually as desirable as those generated by referrals. Leads from referrals were always the most desirable and highest on the scale.

Then I was told, "You know what you need to do, Brian? You need to promote yourself! You need to advertise!" Here was a whole new wastebasketful of opportunities to spend money. I could buy a personal brochure of myself, put my name on signs or run ads in the newspaper or in real estate magazines.

There are as many ways to advertise in real estate as there are inventive or desperate agents. I've even seen my associates buy a bench ad at a bus stop. But every time I saw one of their ads on the bench, there seemed to be a homeless person sleeping on it. That seemed to me to convey the opposite of the message the advertiser wanted to convey.

I learned that you can spend a lot of money trying to generate leads through advertising. However, for me it proved to be another remarkably passive method when it came to actual sales. My own experience and that of my colleagues demonstrated a disappointing result. Over time, we realized a very small percentage of returns from any ad.

These were the methods presented to me as tradition- ally sound, tried and true. If you worked hard enough at any of them, there was a minimal pay-off. You could certainly achieve some sales by using the passive methods. But not consistently or dependably. The few pro-active systems, such as door-knocking and cold-calling, prompted you to do things you didn't want to force on people. I was trapped in a dilemma deriving from traditional approaches that didn't work for me!

There was also a peculiar problem of this day and age to make things more difficult. It's called *cocooning,* and it makes many sales and marketing approaches ineffective. In order to gain privacy, many people tend to hole up at home or work and make access to them difficult. Answering machines, voice mail, and e-mail screen their messages and protect their privacy. And this attitude carries into all aspects of life. They retreat into their castle and pull up the moat, so to speak. It's a tough thing to get by, so make sure your marketing and sales methods aren't obsolete.

Let me assure you that I worked hard at real estate. When you're here as an immigrant, you have no choice but to succeed, so I went after it with all my energy. By the end of my second year in business, I had put up some good sales numbers. I was winning lots of plaques, trophies, and local awards. People were calling me a superstar...on a local basis. My industry was proud of me: "Brian, you're a top producer, and here are all these awards to tell clients how good you are."

I'd made it! Top of the heap, Mom! Member of the Million Dollar Club!

That was very gratifying until I discovered I was spending as much money as I was making, an easy thing to do in real estate sales. I was working seven days a week, and the rest of the time I was on call. I used to sleep with the pager by my bed. Awards notwithstanding, I found myself to be largely disorganized. Although I was grossing a lot of money, I wasn't netting a lot of income. In fact, I wasn't keeping much of what I was making. At the end of my second year came another hard lesson: I discovered the effect of Income Tax on my return for seven-days-a-week effort.

On top of all that, I wasn't enjoying my career because I'd made a big mistake in dealing with clients. In my headlong quest for success, I worked with anybody who wanted to buy or sell a home. I didn't discriminate. If anyone had a down payment for a house, they qualified with me as a potential buyer and, if anyone owned a house, I viewed them as my kind of seller. I'd work with anybody. The problem is, when you're willing to work with anybody, that's who you get. Anybody.

I had some clients who were absolute jackasses. That's the kindest description I can give. I also had many marvelous clients, people it was a pleasure to serve. These were the ones who truly appreciated the excellent service I gave them. I formed a strong relationship with these people because they wanted to be served by someone who gave them a high level of service, personalized care, and integrity.

The best people were easy to deal with. The jackasses were difficult. In fact, for me the jackasses had become the squeaky wheel; they got the grease...more of my time, energy, and effort than anybody. I'd be working with five great clients and, at the same time, have a sixth who was a jackass. That sixth client would take more of my time than the other five combined. My energy and effort were being wasted on the worst client. Over time, the situation became unbearable. So I decided to change my thinking.

I'd been working hard, and there's no doubt that working hard brings you a certain level of achievement. **But hard work alone is no guarantee of success.** Now, I know Americans find that statement hard to swallow. Americans believe that hard work is a virtue and a virtual necessity. Well, it certainly is better than laziness. However, it is not a guarantee of success and specifically not of financial success. I'd been working hard, but not working smart. I'd never asked myself the essential business questions: Whom do I want to serve? What kind of client do I want? What kind of business do I want? What do I want to achieve? As a consequence, I had no plan, no direction, no system...and no answers to these questions.

Despite my trophies and awards and plaques, I felt like a bit of a fraud because my quality of life didn't come up to the general perception of me. Yes, I drove a nice car and wore nice clothes. Yes, my colleagues considered me successful. But I wasn't happy with myself, and I didn't like the way I was doing business. On top of that, my family life was being short-changed. And so, at the end of that second year, I took some time off to consider my business and my future.

> The most important question to ask on the job is not "What am I getting?"
> The most important question to ask is :
> "What am I becoming?"
>
> Unless you change how you are, you will always have what you've got.
> — Jim Rohn

CHAPTER 2

A look in the mirror at myself

When I stepped back and truly looked at myself and my progress in business, I didn't like what I saw.

"Moling" is a catchword I like to use. It describes perfectly what I had been doing. Dig, dig, dig all the time. Go to work, work hard, and dig every day. One day, I popped out of the grass and asked myself, "Where am I, and whose lawn is this?" That's what had happened to me. I'd put my head down like a mole and worked very hard, but I had no idea where I was or how I got there. It was obvious that I needed to regroup, analyze what it was I wanted for my family and myself, and determine what I had to do to fulfill our hopes and dreams.

Some of my questions to myself were immediately answerable. I wanted to build a business that I enjoyed, that gave me pleasure in the doing. And I started to think it through. Exactly what is it I truly enjoy? Well, I really enjoyed sales.

I liked putting a sale together and feeling the energy from that. I loved serving people who appreciated what I'd done for them and for whom I'd made a difference. I liked having no limit on how much I could make. I wanted to run a business that had the potential to be highly profitable. I wanted it to create a platform for me to be successful to my own concept of success. I liked the freedom of my own schedule and being my own boss. And I wanted challenge. I needed interpersonal challenge to keep me sharp and committed and to satisfy my people-person needs.

All these things were good and uplifting, but there was a downside as well. The toughest issues had to do with clients. From experience, I knew I'd have lots of good ones, but what to do with the really bad clients? How could I distance myself from the clients that sapped my time and energy and motivation? How could I eliminate the incompatible ones and find a way to generate more good clients? How could I get more referrals from them?

I racked my brain for realistic answers, considering every approach and possibility. Were there books I could read by anyone who'd built a similar business and been successful? What tapes could I listen to? What seminars or classes could I take? Was there anyone who qualified as a mentor? Did I know anyone who had been successful in overcoming the same kind of business problems? Who could I utilize as a model for my actions?

I thought and thought and over-thought all this for quite a while. Then it came to me, suddenly, in a BFO - a Blinding Flash of the Obvious. I thought of someone I wanted to emulate in business. I came up with the perfect person as a model for my approach to the business of real estate...or for any business. It was my own father. My dad was a painter and decorator. He had a business that was handed on to him by his father, and his father before him, and so on for five generations. Throughout the course of his career, my father always had a lot of work and a lot of men working for him. He never ran an ad, never knocked on a door to get the work, and never called on a previous client. Not one time! How did the work come?

My father, George, and my grandfather, Harry Buffini, depended on a simple principle for their business. At the end of every workday, they toured the job site and, after inspecting your work, they asked a single question: "Can you put your name to that?" If you couldn't, you had to do the work over. They were also tacitly asking: "Would you put my name to it?" As a consequence, their work was outstanding, and they were great business people for this reason. They knew that if you could put your name to your work, you would exceed your client's expectations. The ultimate result was that your client would exceed your expectations by referring you to others for similar work.

> **Let the work speak for itself.**
> — George Buffini, my father

It worked very well indeed for my father and granddad. They had a steady stream of jobs that never seemed to end. The business was run out of our home, and we got phone calls every day. Potential clients asked to speak to Mr. Buffini and said they were referred by someone for whom Mr. Buffini had done work. That was the only way they did business. Quality of work was the reason for the referrals. Word-of-mouth made it go. My father's commitment to excellence in his work impressed me greatly.

It all made great sense, but I simply didn't have the time to wait for that kind of cycle to take hold for me. I'd grown accustomed to food with my meals. My wife and I had gotten used to meeting the mortgage and car payments. There were other financial pressures, personal and business ones, some unforeseeable and some self-inflicted. I have no doubt that most people in business make short-term decisions based on short-term cash flow problems. I know because I had felt forced to make those kinds of decisions in my past. That was something I had to change with a conscious effort and by finding a better way to do business.

> **A man's fortune must be first changed from within.**
> — Chinese Proverb

CHAPTER 3
Re-examining referrals

Here's how it came about for me. I started to examine the way my father and grandfather had built their business. I asked myself how I could apply their principles to myself and my business. Then I considered ways to speed up and focus the process. How could I improve it for my own purposes?

The fact of the matter is my father and grandfather had developed a wonderful business, but it had a major shortcoming; it depended on word-of-mouth, and word-of-mouth is a passive way of marketing. They never knew who was going to call or when. The only thing they had done to cause a referral was a great job. There were people they had done a great job for who never sent them a referral. Of course, there were many who did. But my father and grandfather had no handle on it. They never could be certain how many referrals would come in during any given month. Or how to actually cause more to come in when needed. They had a word-of-mouth business. Passive!

Most people think of *referral* and *word-of-mouth* as the same thing. When you're given a referral, you've got good word-of-mouth, and when you have good word-of-mouth, you get referrals. There's a certain truth to that. People do get business by word-of-mouth, and they get referrals from those sources: people tell other people. Let me tell you that these terms are not the same, and they are not interchangeable.

Maybe you've had this experience. Someone calls you and says: "Hi, Brian...bumped into Billy the other day. He and his wife are thinking about selling their home and buying another. I gave them your card and told them to call you." And those people have never contacted you. This is typical of the ineffectiveness of passive word-of-mouth. How many times do you think there's been a conversation on your behalf that you don't even know about?

Realizing this, I immediately made a conscious choice for pro-active methods in my new approach to business. Passive ways are not and will never be my style; there are too many disadvantages. You sit around and wait for someone to call you. You feel out-of-control with your business and your revenue stream. You don't know who you're going to serve or when. You may get a rush of clients, all at the same time, which overloads your capabilities. Passive is a more chaotic and disorganized way of doing business. It causes you to live in fear, wondering where your next lead will come from. Too many uncertainties! The fear causes bad business practices.

Many people believe that they'll get a referral when they hand out a business card. They meet someone, have a conversation, and end it with: "If you know anyone who needs my services..." and bring out the old dependable business card. If you're hoping to get referrals from that, you're a great optimist. In fact, it requires four separate and distinct miracles for a referral to result from a business card:

Miracle # 1: The recipient of the card has to keep it and not lose it.

Miracle # 2: The person to whom you originally gave the card has to have it in hand when encountering a friend or acquaintance who actually needs your services.

Miracle # 3: The friend or acquaintance has to not lose the card and has to remember where it came from. If they can't recall who gave them the card, a week later it's just another business card in the purse or wallet, eventually to be thrown away.

Miracle # 4: The friend or acquaintance has to remember and find the card when they're ready to call for the services you provide.

If you've handed out business cards and gotten referrals from them on a regular basis, it's incredible! It shows that God loves you because He has provided four miracles for your business on multiple occasions.

From another perspective, consider how many referrals are actually out there. If you've gotten a few referrals from business cards, it's like finding two stray ants in your kitchen; it's not the two ants that excite you, it's the possibility that there are a million ants nearby that you haven't seen. Limited by the business-card mentality, there are a million referrals nearby that you haven't tapped into!

There are many ways to ruin potential referrals by alienating clients, and most salespeople aren't even aware that they're shooting themselves in the foot. I've seen people in all kinds of businesses constantly overlook their current clients while they look for the next client. That's the fastest way I know to end up with no clients. I see it as a challenge and a necessity to deliver a high level of service to people; and to do it in such a way that it exceeds their expectations; and delights them; so they are brimming over to tell their friends about the exceptional service they received and from whom.

When I recently bought a new car, I could tell the automobile salespeople were so determined to make a sale that no other aspect of the process had any meaning for them. It didn't matter to them what they sold, where it was going, whether or not it was the right car for me. It was apparent the only thing that concerned them was making the deal. They brought out the awful

27

qualities of a mishandled word-of-mouth business. The process was not pleasant, smooth or enjoyable. It was ugly, and it left me cold. Because of that, even though the automobile they sold me is excellent, I would never refer anyone to them. I wouldn't want a friend of mine to go through that process. If I did tell friends about the product, I'd say the dealership sells great cars, but I'd let them know it's not pleasant to buy a car there. That would be as negative a referral as I can imagine.

In the course of my rethinking, I tried to consider everything, good and bad, that affects people's choices in business. It struck me that accelerating technology had become an important factor. In this age of technology, many people are confused by it and lose the true sense of how to conduct business. While the Internet and messaging tools of today are great aids to us, they do not create personal service. In fact, they are often depersonalizing. And they cannot replace the essential human considerations and practices upon which business and personal relationships are based.

I make that point in my seminars, and I relate it specifically to business referrals. For example, I often ask the ladies in the audience, "Where did you go to get your hair done?" I follow up with, "Did you find your hairdresser on the Internet? Did you go to an open salon day? Did a telemarketer call you at night during dinner to ask if you were interested in getting your hair done?"

They always laugh at the ridiculousness of the question, but it makes a point that is supremely important to my philosophy of business: the ladies go where others have personally assured them they'll find a good stylist and get a good job. They'll ask a friend they trust. They want a referral because it's important to them how their hair looks.

In sales, most people sell something far more important and expensive than a haircut. If people seek a referral for a hair stylist, how much more do they want a referral when they're in need of more costly services.

People are always looking for someone to trust. It's human nature to search and ask for referrals. And we're eager to share our find. The urge to refer friends and family to someone we trust is also part of our nature. No matter what technology or sophisticated tool is developed...no matter how all-pervasive the Internet becomes, personal referral will remain the single most persuasive selling tool in business. Personal referral based on trust will never go out of style.

CHAPTER 4
Developing Trust

Trust is the key component to doing business by referral. In order to get referrals from people, you must have their trust. There's more to it than you may think. Most people equate trust with character one-dimensionally. They regard it strictly as the ethical product of a person's character. That's only half of it! There's also the trust that stems from competence, equally important in business. Your character may be above reproach, but if you screw up deals for clients, you probably won't earn their trust or receive their referrals. It's that simple. However, it's sometimes difficult to get clients to assess competence and character because of their one-dimensional perspective. And they may not recognize your competence readily.

It's extremely important to communicate both, and I relate the following true story to prove it.

Across the country every year, I teach thousands of sales people how to do business by referral. People from the mortgage, loan, and insurance businesses also attend my seminars. Several years ago, Ron, a very competent real estate agent, in the business for nine years, came to the program. This fine man, of excellent character and very good at what he did, told me this story during one of the breaks.

He had led a weekly Bible study class in his community for years. A gentleman in the class was having significant problems with his teenage kids, and Ron was concerned for him. Ron and his wife had raised a family successfully, so they offered to meet with the troubled couple for counseling two to three times a week for four or five months. The counseling helped immensely. Two years later, the counseled couple were transferred out of town. Surprisingly, they put their home on the market with another realtor. In fact, they listed it with an agent from the same office as Ron. Crestfallen by their apparent slight, Ron came to me looking for advice.

My answer was, "I'll give you the advice that my wife Beverly gave me a few years ago," and I told him what happened when I complained to Beverly about some problem I was experiencing at the time. She responded with a large, colorful sticker which she placed on top of the bathroom mirror on my side. Beverly believes that I am entitled to her opinion, and she gives it freely. I went into the bathroom, looked in the mirror, and read: *You are now looking at the problem.*

I looked Ron in the eye and said, "You're the problem. Do you think that couple trusted your character?"

He replied, "Absolutely. They did. They know me. They trusted me with helping them raise their kids."

I said, "Then the problem was they didn't know about your competence."

That was intensely frustrating to him because he is a highly competent agent. It points out how difficult it is to communicate your own character and competence to someone else. It is very difficult to convey that yourself...but it is not difficult for someone else to communicate it for you.

That's the unique impact of the referral. It takes someone other than yourself to verify your character and competence and create trust with immediate credibility. It's difficult to do that yourself without appearing boastful. Human nature makes the referral totally objective and effective. In a conversation with your potential client, a third party can establish with ease both your character and your competence. I was getting closer to an innovative way to cause such conversations. My goal was to essentially turn clients into "walkin' talkin' billboards" for my business and me.

The beauty of my father as a model was that I could see the strengths and weaknesses of his business because I knew it so well. His value as a mentor came by learning from his sound work ethic and from his striving for excellence to please his clients. I decided to build my business with that same level of service and commitment to the client, exceeding their expectations.

However, I realized that I needed more dependable ways to generate business than word-of-mouth.

I was almost there. I knew that referrals didn't have to be passively waited for. I was convinced you could cause them predictably. I was determined to **generate referrals pro-actively**. I wanted to actually cause those referrals to happen at their source, and I wanted to know how many I would get each month. All I had to do now was create the processes to constantly spark referrals...and put them into my business...to get choice clients to refer me...because of my character and competence...in specific ways...to new, potentially choice clients...who would become sources of referral. Well, let's revise that to: I was almost there, with a lot of details to figure out...

I consider a referral to be both cause and effect. It's what you're after, and it's what you need in order to get what you're after. In another sense, it has caused the major shift in my business life and has had the effect of making everything easier and better. My financial fortunes radically changed, and my entire life improved, all because I took the time to think about a pro-active system that generated referrals at their source. I believe my most significant career accomplishment was learning to think from the perspective of the long-term. It prompted me to view my clients relationally instead of transactionally.

CHAPTER 5
The lost art of Service

As my thinking and my commitment to a referral-driven business evolved, I realized I'd have to consider all the different areas of the business, client motivation, and personal communication techniques in order to make this referral thing a reality.

I dedicated myself to covering all the bases and coming up with accomplishable answers to every aspect. My first consideration was service. Here, in a nutshell, is what came of some very heavy thinking on my part about service.

People have to have a compelling reason to refer you. You must provide a specific, unique service with value that inspires people to tell others about you and your business. Your service must be controllable, constant and consistent. Therefore, it has to be organized, structured and systematized. It can't be something you happened to provide coincidentally on a good day. If people entrust friends to you because of the quality of your service, they must be certain those friends will get the same level of service that they received.

> **McDonald's is successful because they are consistent.**

This was not a difficult commitment for me. As a youngster watching my father's business, I had witnessed the sustaining effects of dedication to higher service. As a teenager working for him, I had redone more than a few days' work to meet his high standards. It was ingrained in me. From the outset of my real estate career, I cared for my clients and had always tried to provide the highest level of service and value to them. Now that I was rethinking my approach to business, dedication to effective service became the primary building block in the process.

We all know of certain businesses that put out the best product and deliver exceptional service. Because of that, one person tells another, and they're always flooded with customers.

For me, one of the best examples is a seafood restaurant in the middle of Nowhere, Illinois. It's in the boondocks and not exactly adjacent to either ocean, yet it's become one of the top five restaurants in the U.S. They have 630 tables, and on Mother's Day, they'll turn those tables six times in the day. This is unheard of for a seafood restaurant! On most mid-days and evenings, the restaurant is extremely crowded. On Saturday nights, there's usually a two-hour wait in line. Two hours, in the middle of nowhere! And this is not the least expensive place in the world! So how do they do it? Why do people flock to them? What makes people bring thermoses to sip while they stand in line for two hours on a chilly Saturday evening in October in the boondocks in the middle of the country, as I did? It's not for the fine china or linen napkins; this place doesn't have any. The food is superb, but the customers come for more than that. Inside, the service is spectacular; the drinks are wonderful, especially the trademark Mai Tai's. The customers flock to the place because the entire dining experience is a pleasure. The owner has anticipated their every need, want, and comfort...except for the unavoidable wait in line. The restaurant has succeeded because he exceeds their expectations; because he serves his customers to their needs and perspective, not his own. Because of his commitment to service.

The restaurant is constantly crowded because everyone who goes there recommends it enthusiastically to everyone they know. And that reputation for service was what I wanted for my business.

In keeping with my own philosophy of referral, I must tell you that the name of this superb place is Bob Chin's Seafood Restaurant in Wheeling, Illinois. If you're ever around Chicago, be sure to go there.

It wasn't enough to roll out the red carpet for clients; it had to go beyond that; and it had to be natural, personalized, and continuing. I wanted the commitment to service to display my esteem for them beyond what anyone else in the business provided. I thought of it as *client appreciation.*

Furthermore, I wanted my clients to know, understand and appreciate that. Now what was the best way to get it across to them? After thinking it through, the answer was simple: I had to tell them what I was doing.

It felt right and good to start by stating my complete commitment to my clients. Stating the commitment was crucial to starting the process. At the same time, I could foresee that it would be rewarding to me. I'd tell them I was going to entrust my business to them and that I was going to do it by offering them a new, deeper level of service. I'd explain my methods simply and completely, state my total commitment to doing business exclusively by referral, and make them understand their importance to me. I would explain to them how I did business...that I had to do a great job for them because, if I didn't, I wouldn't get any referrals; and if I didn't get any referrals, my business would dry up.

To be completely honest, the first time I stated my commitment to a client, I felt a twinge of fear. I found it a bit nerve-racking to think that my business would depend entirely on my clients. There was the feeling that I'd given over control. It's a leap of faith for most people, and it was for me at the beginning. Don't forget, this was uncharted territory for me, as it will be for you.

After the fact, it turned out to be a great comfort to my clients. They heard my words as: "Hey, if I don't do a great job for you, I'm not going to end up with much business." This involved and empowered them in their dealings with me. And it's a good thing that they were empowered by my commitment to them because my entire business model was built on the belief that they would send me referrals.

When it comes to commitment, my wife, Beverly, is a shining example and my greatest teacher. Bev earned All-American honors as a volleyball player at the University of Tennessee, where they later retired her jersey. After college, she went on to represent the United States as a member of the U. S. National Team that played in the Olympics at Seoul in 1988. Beverly showed me what it took to be an Olympic-caliber achiever. To become an Olympic volleyball player, she dedicated herself to work within a system.

She made a commitment to do the ordinary drills and skill practices so consistently that she would become extraordinary. Beverly gave maximum effort and focus to the ordinary drills every day, no matter how basic and simple, no matter how monotonous. She made the commitment that, any time a ball was hit in her direction, it would never hit the ground. She made the commitment to chase down every loose ball hit in her direction; to jump high and strong in every drill; to run hard and fast in every sprint every day. And she kept to it in every drill, every single day. Beyond what the coaches directed her to do in a rigorous full-time schedule, she made a commitment to herself to do a personal program of exercises and activities, and she stuck to it without wavering.

Bev became an outstanding Olympic athlete by never taking her foot off the gas, consistently sticking to her basic plan. I have been greatly influenced by her commitment and drive, and I put those same principles to work for myself.

Commitment is crucial in my referral system. You have to reach a point in your thinking where you are determined to make the commitment to your clients and tell them about it. That's why my system isn't for everyone. After weighing all the information carefully, you have to be the kind of person who states positively, "I want to do business by referral because I believe referrals are the best way to go." Your commitment must be wholehearted, and you must be prepared to turn up your level of service and give clients the first-class treatment they deserve and respond to. That's exactly the commitment I had to make when I began this process. And it has been well repaid with referral after referral after referral.

CHAPTER 6
You gotta have a system

So there I was, committed to the concept of running my business completely by referral. I had done the preliminary thinking and was ready to start. I knew that I had to devise a structured system, work within it, and stick to it.

I cannot stress enough that for most people success requires planning, system, and commitment.

Perhaps a fortunate few can make it without these essentials, but it became obvious to me that I was not among those lucky lottery winners. Fortunately, I learned this as a hard lesson when I ended up moling and unhappy as a result of my haphazard early efforts in the business. It was fortunate because I was young enough to correct my mistake. And it was fortunate that I had Beverly as a model. I continue to marvel at her devotion to planning and system in everyday life, and her adherence to system and schedule. Living with Beverly has taught me many things that I have put into my thinking and my business.

Without planning, you do not have a system. Without commitment, you cannot make a system work. Without a system, you do not have a business...or a life. Without working within a system in business, you're a loose cannon, affected by things you didn't plan for and can't control, damaging your chances for success.

The truth of that philosophy is obvious. Consider the fact that even nature operates with systems within a larger system. If I'd been smarter and more experienced when I was younger, I'd have seen the need for systems by the countless examples of successful people in all fields, astronauts to athletes, Neil Armstrong to Lance Armstrong to Madame Curie to Allen Greenspan. But I was too active and too driven to stop and think it all out. I had confused activity with accomplishment. However, in a strange way, that brought me to understand the crying need to systematize my business as well as my personal life.

> Action, to be effective, must be directed to clearly conceived ends.
> — Nehru

As I started to figure it all out, a droll story about systems came to mind:

A young man sat on a bench in a park, talking to himself, pondering the mysteries of life and success. Just as the young man asked himself the question, "What is the main ingredient of success in life?", a homeless person sat down on the bench next to him.

"System!", the homeless man said forcefully. "You gotta have a system." He surprised the young man who turned to look at him and saw that the answer had come from a ragged, bearded man holding a garbage bag half-full of odds and ends. "You gotta plan everything out and build a smart system with solid structure. You gotta operate within that structure and stick to it. I started my own business, and that's what I did."

"That sounds good, but you obviously have nothing," the young man said. "What happened?"

"I'll tell ya for a quarter." The homeless man stood up, smiled, shifted his garbage bag, and stuck out his hand.

The young man reached in his pocket for a quarter, put it in the outstretched palm, and inquired, "Well?"

"My system didn't work!"

That wasn't going to happen to me. My system would work. I'd make sure with careful planning and smart thinking. I'd prove its feasibility at every step along the way.

As I've stated in regard to service, you must provide a controllable, constant and consistently high level; therefore, your efforts have to be organized, structured and systematized. I took my own advice and took the time to plan how and where I should invest my efforts and resources to achieve this. I wrote down my goals. I considered all the possibilities and problems that might come in building a real estate business that ran solely on referrals. I discussed it and consulted with everyone who could contribute experience and knowledge. I ended up with a solid plan, and from that plan I devised the basic structure of my referral system. The entire process clarified my thinking and gave me strength and confidence in what I was doing.

I created a system for generating referrals. It is a human system designed to be implemented and applied seriously within a program that requires strategy, commitment, and consistent application by people like you. **My system is engineered for specific psychological reaction and response and to meet interactive human needs.** That's what I designed it to do.

Each element and action I put forward in this system has been carefully considered, tested over time, and proved effective. And the system works to maximum efficiency when the elements are correctly combined, applied and sequenced with the proper motivation. **Trust the system and work the system.**

When people refer you, they validate your working system.

Referrals System Overview

Here's a graphic example I use in my training seminars to show how the system works. Think of it as a giant orange juice producer, then picture clients as oranges and referrals as the juice.

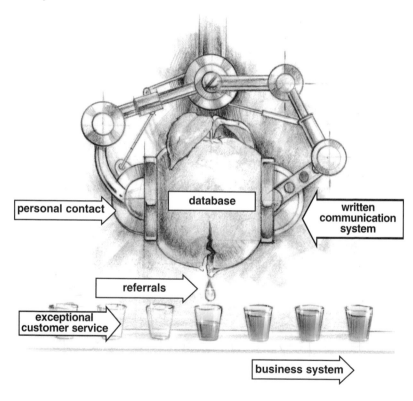

Pour It On!

The constant, growing generation of leads from referrals creates a surplus of transactions. This overflow
gives you more business than you can handle,
enabling you to share the surplus with others.

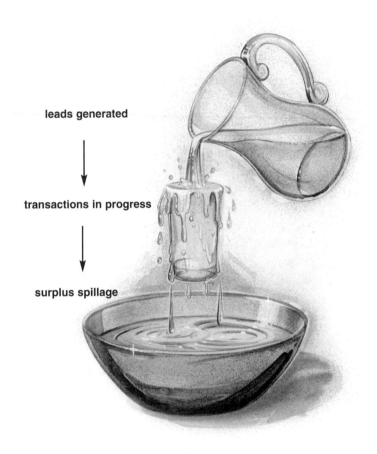

leads generated

transactions in progress

surplus spillage

CHAPTER 7
Choose your own clients

I had done my planning and structure. Now it was time to actually develop the components of that system. I had to choose a solid starting point, and I did what every concerned craftsman does when starting a task: I checked the tools and materials I had to work with. The most prominent and useful was my client list.

What's the natural thing to do when you're facing a decision, deadline or dilemma, and searching for assistance? Most individuals look for help or answers from people they know and trust...family, friends, colleagues and business associates. They leaf through their address books, flip Rolodex cards or scroll through computer lists, looking for the persons they prefer to help them solve their problem. In the process, they inevitably find themselves assessing and prioritizing the people they're reviewing.

Essentially, that's what I did when I began to sort out my business. I sorted through my list of clients. I analyzed my client base to determine exactly who I most wanted to do business with. The list was my primary tool and the most natural starting point. I saw it as necessary to decide up front the clients I wanted on my preferred list. Whom did I want to serve? Who would be a source of referrals?

Which clients would generate the kind of referrals I wanted? And, unfortunately, whom should I exclude? We now call this process **sorting and qualifying your client base.** In the beginning, I called it common sense.

What I did initially by sorting and qualifying my client base turned out to be the most important step I could have taken. It made me evaluate my clients objectively and set me up for success down the line. It is a critical element for anyone who wants to upgrade their business to be driven by referrals.

Starting the process can be aggravating, and for some it can seem overwhelming. So many people; so many factors; so many judgments and choices! I remember my own perplexed feelings about it. I needed to begin with an idea of what made up my ideal client. Who were they? What were they? What kind of people? What did they need and expect from me? What were their financial situations, and what kind of return was I looking for?

From many factors, I attempted to build a model of my ideal client. When I finally got that ideal fixed in my mind, it was amazing how I was able to see and find answers to many of my questions. I was able to find what I was looking for only after I knew what I was looking for. I have a good friend who says, "Most people aim for nothing and hit it with amazing accuracy." I really didn't want to be most people.

My basis for my database was my existing client and contact lists, pretty much everybody I knew in business. I was fortunate to already have a large, significant client list. Many people start by throwing in family, friends, colleagues, everyone they know or remember having met. Unless you're brand new in business, this is not the best way to go about it. Initially, it's better to look at what you already have.

> **Do what you can, with what you have, where you are.**
> — Theodore Roosevelt

Working to my ideal, I started to sort out my preferred clients, those whom I deemed most willing to refer me. Not as easy as it sounds! It takes a great deal of objective work to sort the flowers from the weeds. It's human nature and much easier to think of every person in your garden as a flower and retain every one as preferred. I couldn't afford to think like that. My future depended on sorting and qualifying that database to get it organized, down to the most fundamental group of preferred people.

Think of it as if you owned an airline. You'd necessarily have to sort and qualify your passengers. You'd have to know who were first class, who traveled in coach, and who used your airline mainly to ship freight. In the process, you'd discover who were your frequent fliers, who really filled your seats and were worth your space.

Airlines must make this evaluation, and all businesses should. The results are usually surprising and enlightening. All the companies I've dealt with have something in common: no matter how large or small the business, 80% of the revenue stems from less than 20% of the clients. The trick, and the necessity, is to know who they are. Then we can focus our efforts on these vital, dependable clients with service and attention that keeps them ecstatic. So they become "walkin' talkin' billboards" for us. That's what we're trying to achieve.

I set up four categories for my client list: A, B,C and D. It makes sorting easy, and I recommend you do the same.

"A" people are those who are **most willing** to send you a referral. The key phrase here is *most willing*. They don't have to be someone who sent you a referral in the past. They don't necessarily have to be someone with whom you've done business. They do have to be the people who are most sold on you, those you believe to be totally on your team. Since you don't want to presume this, you need to call and ask: "Would you like to be on my preferred client list?" Briefly explain what that entails:

"These are special people like you who are going to be sending referrals to me throughout the year, and I want to do some extra-special things for them on a regular basis." Your "A" clients then are the people most willing to refer you, and they have verified their interest and involvement by affirming it to you.

"B" people in your database are those who would refer you, if asked, and shown how. They are persons in your sphere of influence or in your business network. In your sphere of influence, they are folks you know personally, including friends and acquaintances. In your business network, they are associates or people you do business with. This includes accountants or attorneys or anyone whose services you utilize. You may be a client of theirs, or they may be a client of yours. And don't forget people in the supporting trades. You never know when a painter or decorator or carpenter may be the source of a superlative referral.

"C" clients are people who are new to your database. They may refer you in the future. They're persons you've just met and added to your list. You're not sure how they stack up, but you want to consider them within your database.

"D" stands for "delete". These are the people you do not want to do business with...the jackasses and jerks who prove to be a waste of your time and energy. Or those who are simply a bad fit for you personally or profit-wise. "D" people are the logical fall-out when you go through your database and react by thinking: "I truly don't want to do business with these people or any people they might steer my way." It's not personal or an act of malice on your part. It's simply being objective and practical, making a choice of the kind of client you want. To optimize your business, you've chosen to focus your efforts on "A" people. Everyone else is "B" or "C" or deleted. **Deleting is of utmost importance in establishing and maintaining your database.** It is as necessary to successful growth as pruning a tree.

We want to retain the "B" and "C" people in the database. Obviously, the goal is to turn C's into B's and B's into A's over time. If uncertain about someone, contact the person and sound them out. If the initial database is too large to do that, send out letters designed to help those people self-select. If the initial database is sparse or small, call each person and ask if they'd be interested in being one of your preferred clients. Ask if you're someone they'd refer in the future? If they say, "Absolutely no," delete 'em.

As you select and delete, don't be intimidated if the list shrinks dramatically. One of the first couples we ever coached at Providence Systems, Sam and Edith Elzie from Bear, Delaware, had 440 people in their initial database. The year before they joined Providence, they had made only 13 sales. After we helped them sort and qualify their database down to 42 "A" clients, using the system, they generated 308 referrals the next year. Size isn't what counts; it's quality of client. Keep the original focus. Sort and qualify to get your "A" people.

There are several points I want to make about using and refining your database, and they are best illustrated by a discussion of gold-mining methods. Prospecting is an interesting term applied to sales. It refers to gold mining and has come to describe the way to find new leads.

The Gold Rushes in California and Alaska were started when gold was discovered along streams and riverbeds. Early prospectors painstakingly panned by hand for gold in the rivers and streams. It didn't take them long to improve the process by constructing sluices. They built wooden channels that directed the water to push rock, sand, and gravel through a sluice. This washed away and reduced the unwanted rubble and deposited the heavier metal, gold, where it was more apparent. Prospectors sat at the end of the sluice, sorting through the reduced sand, rock, and rubble to pick out bits and nuggets of gold. It was a much more productive system than panning by hand.

Here's my point: prospecting is primarily finding the best way to sort through what you already have. If you're smart and experienced, you use natural flow and force to work for you. In the real estate business, instead of water, the force comes from the people who are most willing and eager to send you referrals. Harness the power of that stream by building your database correctly, and you'll find gold in the form of "A" people.

My next point is this: in order to make gold more valuable, you refine it. The more you refine gold, the more valuable it becomes. You've sorted out your "A" people, so you know who your best clients are. They're your separated gold. Most of them have probably been the source of a referral. Now you have to come up with another category for those people who have sent you multiple referrals. Call it "A+". These are your Super A's. Make a special effort to find and identify them. They are nuggets of purer gold and deserving of special attention. While all your "A" people go first class on your airline, Super A's get V.I.P. treatment. This means you give them the most of your time, energy, and specific attention. You go out of your way for them and do extra-special things, no matter how busy or successful your business becomes. If you don't do that, somebody else will. As you build your database, focus on them first and foremost.

Normally, when an "A" client referred someone to me, the next day I would send them a personal handwritten thank-you note and enclose a gift certificate for dinner for two. That was to thank them for their endorsement of me. I wanted to show them how much I appreciated the high compliment they had paid me by putting their name to mine. It is, after all, the supreme compliment you can receive.

Some of my "A+" clients sent me referral after referral after referral. How did I acknowledge that? In twelve months, one particular "A+" client, Andy Peterson, sent nineteen referrals that closed for me. You can bet I did more for Andy than just send him a gift certificate for dinner. He personified the client who deserved my special attention and treatment. This is the client I take to dinner; I go out of my way to do special things for him and his family; and I encourage him every way I can in his business and life. The least I can do is try to be as big a blessing to him as he has been to me.

This referral system is built out of an abundance mentality. It's a wonderful way to do business. **When you give to a giver, a giver gives back. And when you give more to a giver, they give back even more!** Conversely, when you give to a taker, they just take. In my system, I give to the givers, and the takers get deleted. I spent my days only with good folks, people I was happy to talk to, like Andy Peterson, and they were happy to hear from me. I never felt like I was imposing myself. I enjoyed doing business by referral because I enjoyed the people I was working with, and I enjoyed the referrals they sent me. And it all began with my existing client list.

Let's look at the power of your database and its ability to connect in this referral system. According to the Gallup Poll, the average American knows approximately 285 people. That means each of your "A" clients knows around 285 people. That's a lot of people! Multiply 285 times the number of your "A" clients, and the potential number of referrals is staggering. As an actual example, I had 300 "A" people in my database. Conservatively, let's say that each knew only 100 people. That's 30,000 potential referrals!

The beautiful thing about this process is its interconnectivity. It's a two-way street. I was only one conversation away from Andy Peterson and all the people he knows. The same was true of each of the 300 "A" people in my database. I was tapped into a massive number of people, and each person was a potential referral.

Just as importantly, each was a warm lead who knew of me through my "A" people. When someone came to me by referral, it was through the filter of my 300 "A" people. I could be virtually certain that the referral would be good because my clients would never intentionally send me a bad client. They were eager to send me someone good who belonged in first class with them. So I not only tapped into a huge number of potential referrals, but each actual referral was pre-qualified for me. That is the simplified explanation for the immediate exponential growth of my production in real estate. It also accounts for the high quality of clients and the ability to deliver exceptional service. These are the benefits of business by referral.

The ultimate goal in utilizing your database is to create what I call "critical mass." In sales and marketing, critical mass is the immediate popular association of a certain product or service with a specific person or company. The effect is self-sustaining. For example, I mention tissues, and what company instantly comes to mind? Kleenex. I use the copy machine, and I instinctively think Xerox. Through dedication to system and service, you can create critical mass for yourself and your business. I achieved critical mass with 300 "A" people, including 18 "A+" clients, and it was extremely satisfying and rewarding.

It is a costly mistake to think that the only ones who matter in your client base are those you've directly helped to buy or sell a home. Many times in my career I received a highly profitable referral from someone I'd never done business with personally. I had never helped them buy or sell a home, yet they became wonderful sources of business for me. That's what this is all about...sorting out the individuals we should appreciate most. In this referral system, the quality of the person is the primary consideration. We want to do business with people of quality, those who will appreciate our efforts and respond. Sorting and qualifying our client list means that we can direct our personal attention to this select group of people. More focus and attention on fewer people will produce incredible results for your business.

CHAPTER 8
Something of value

When I was done with the database, my next task was to find a way to appropriately express my appreciation to clients. I couldn't paint all their houses or wash 300 cars every month. I had already developed the practice of thanking people for referrals by sending them a hand-written note and a dinner-for-two gift certificate. That had been well-received, but I was determined to do more for my "A" clients on a constant basis. And I wanted to spark their response and referrals with whatever the expression of appreciation would be.

It would have to be personal and/or professional in nature with interesting value to the recipient. It would have to have substance in a form that my clients could touch, hold, see or hear, enjoy and appreciate; and in a form that I could deliver or send monthly by mail.

It would have to be variable, generally appealing, and manageable because I planned to furnish it on a consistent monthly basis to a large number of people, and I didn't want it to be repetitive or boring. I wanted it to be uniquely from me. And it would be doubly grand if it could communicate my character and competence.

After some trial and error, I came up with **Items of Value**, a varied menu of thoughtful gifts, entertainments, information, and economies. I provided these Items of Value to my "A" clients every month, and the procedure became known as my *Client Appreciation Program*. Moreover, I divided the items into two groupings: Personal Items to communicate my character and Professional Items to convey my competence. I mixed and matched and alternated the items to achieve a consistent balance between character and competence.

The personal items were inventive and varied and often brought me great enjoyment, like when I sent flowers for Mother's Day to the preferred people in my database. Sometimes I would arrange a get-together for my clients. I'd rent an entire movie theater for a mid-week performance at a bargain group-rate and invite all my clients. Once a year for Valentine's night, I held a Sweetheart Banquet. We'd have couples get together at a local restaurant. They paid ten dollars, and I subsidized the rest for all of us to get together for dinner. After dinner, we picked couples' names to play our version of the Newlywed Game. My clients just loved this. They had a great time getting together. They also loved the raffles. I'd buy tickets for front-row seats to a hit show such as *Riverdance* or *Phantom of the Opera* and hold a raffle for my "A" people. With this month's Item of Value, we'd announce the raffle and tell them to check next month's Item of Value for the winners. People really got into it, and many called to ask who won.

The one-cent stamp is a classic example of the effectiveness of a simple, inexpensive Item of Value. It was a stroke of genius from a realtor enrolled in the Providence program. This little personal item cost hardly anything, but showed clients the realtor was thinking about them and their needs. When the U. S. Postal Service changed the rate for a first-class letter from 32 to 33 cents, he sent his clients a page of one-cent stamps. Along with it, he enclosed the message: *"I'm here for you, even for the small stuff."*
— The-one-cent stamp Item of Value was originated by Paul Moore, Tempe, Arizona

Sometimes we'd tailor the personal item to a seasonal event, as we did with the printed sheet, *How to make going back to school less stressful on your child*. We sent that out late in August, just before the kids were going back to school. Parents and grandparents appreciated and shared the suggestions with their children. On the personal side, let me also point out that Items of Value can be used selectively when someone in your database needs comforting or encouragement. The item might be something as simple as a poem. When I knew people were dealing with change in their lives, I sent them a copy of Robert Frost's *The Road Not Taken.*

On the professional side, we developed Items of Value that pertained to: real estate; financial or tax matters; related office and paperwork efficiencies and economies;

news and reviews of regulations, laws, industry changes, associations; and the like. The most popular were those items that put forth ways for people to save money or recommendations that would impact them financially. We did the research and sent clients information sheets on a wide range of practical topics, such as *The Top Ten Mutual Funds, The 25 Most Overlooked Tax Tips, How to Get Out of Consumer Debt*, and *The Top Ten Websites*. Often the item was industry-specific: *How to Accelerate Your Mortgage* or *30 Tips on How to Make Your Home More Sellable*. Informational items like these were of special value to my clients because they could be shared in turn with their own clientele.

I also produced a Referral Directory and sent it to my clients. It alphabetically listed all the good people who had done business with me and whose services I could recommend. My criteria for inclusion were that I had to have done business with the listed party and they had to be good at what they did. The directory contained a description of their business along with contact information, addresses and phone numbers. I made sure it covered every kind of service that would be needed by someone just moving into the area or starting a small business. It included painters, attorneys, accountants, roofers, carpet cleaners, even music teachers. I added listings and sent out supplemental pages periodically, creating an additional Item of Value and a favorable impression of follow-through on my part. The popularity of the directory with my clients proved well worth the effort. Many times when I was in a client's home or office, I'd see my Referral Directory, dog-eared with use, by the telephone. It appeared that my clients used it as much or more than the Yellow Pages.

Each month, I took the time to think of inventive, practical Items of Value that benefited my clients. At the same time, I made certain that these items demonstrated my character and competence. It's a grand idea that works well to everyone's advantage. This is not to say that every Item of Value was a smash hit with my clients. Some items fell a bit short, and a few were total duds, but I learned by my mistakes.

Through the years in my business, I constantly tested and improved the items to improve their acceptance and effectiveness. This process of refinement has been carried forward by the inventive people of Providence Systems and brought to its highest form by many enterprising Providence subscribers. We have the added value and pleasure of sharing the new and the best items with all of our members.

Any way you look at it, the program has always been enthusiastically received, by attendees of our seminars, the people we coach, and by the Providence members and their clients. Its popularity has proven its merit, and

I haven't seen any better way to express client appreciation or to communicate character and competence.

Every month, an Item of Value went out to my 300 clients to express my appreciation of them and to remind them that they were my first-class passengers, uppermost in my consideration and concern. It set up a wonderful opportunity for me to get on the phone with them.

I found that following up the Item of Value each month with a personal telephone call was crucial to maximize the effect of the item. It reinforced that I cared about my clients, and they welcomed my calls. It also gave me a legitimate reason to communicate with them and prompt referrals. I made the commitment to myself to make fifteen phone calls to my database each and every working day, and the monthly item was generally my entree.

I never liked calls out of the blue that were obviously prospecting for business, and I was determined not to do that to my clients. I didn't want to confuse them about my intentions. Yes, I wanted to do a lot of business and I was extremely driven to be successful; however, my primary reason for contacting people was to serve them. I genuinely enjoyed serving people who appreciated being served by me, and I wanted my calls to reflect that:

"Hi, Mary, this is Brian Buffini calling from Buffini Real Estate. I just wanted to check in with you, to see how you

and the family are doing. You know, last week I sent you a page of one-cent stamps in the mail. Did you get that little item?"

"Yes, I did, Brian. I really appreciate that. We already used the stamps. That was very thoughtful of you."

"I'm glad you liked it, Mary. I'm always thinking of ways to serve you, and I thought it was a neat idea to save you the hassle of having to run out and buy stamps. It was just a little gift to show my appreciation."

I was calling people who knew me and with whom I had a relationship. Because of my calling discipline and regularity, they came to know that I was checking to make sure my thoughtfulness had reached them. When I asked if they had received the item of the month, if they replied that they hadn't opened it yet, I urged them to be sure that they opened and used the item. It was understood that I would keep the conversation social and non-threatening. That was a large part of the reason they welcomed my calls and responded well. No one in business wants to hear a stiff-legged sales pitch over the phone, not even from someone they like. I was simply applying the hard lessons I'd learned early in my career from those nasty cold calls.

Applied in a consistent program, the Items of Value build in interest and worth. Beyond their value as an expression of appreciation, the Items of Value provide an excellent means of access to clients. They open doors...and phones...and make clients receptive. The follow-up phone calls become a principal and natural form of communication between us. I call after I've sent them an Item of Value. They're appreciative of it. We're having a nice casual chat. That doesn't mean the conversation can't be directed to harvest referrals from people who are already sold on me. As the culmination of my Client Appreciation Program, do I now jump to a hard-bitten sales pitch? Do I blatantly ask for referrals. No, of course not! I do better than that. Before I finish the conversation and hang up the phone, I say something that has made me a fortune and helped create success for tens of thousands of business professionals I've trained.

CHAPTER 9
Oh, by the way...

We're in the business of generating leads, and we're committed to doing business by referral. Everything we do in this system is designed to generate referrals. Every contact, written communication, and conversation is an opportunity, but you have to know how to ask for referrals. Whenever I'm speaking with a client or with anyone who can provide a referral, I end the conversation with the same simple few sentences:

"Oh, by the way, if you know of anyone who is thinking of buying or selling a home who would appreciate this same level of service, just give me a call with their name and number. I'll be happy to follow up with them for you."

That's how you ask for referrals. And you say this every time you get the opportunity. This simple, innocuous catch-phrase, almost an afterthought, has become the mainstay of my system and a wellspring for referrals. I developed it and refined the words through years of use, and I recommend that you memorize and say it exactly the way it's written here. Just as your appearance and manner shape the client's perception, the right words at the right time are critical to your success.

The words, "Oh, by the way," make a marvelous transition in any conversation, either to change the subject or to conclude the talk. The idea to use these words came while I was watching an episode of Columbo, one of my favorite detective shows. It was his signature line.

Inspector Columbo, rumpled and deferring, investigates puzzling homicides committed by Hollywood highbrows. The killers are usually important, superior people who look down their collective nose at Columbo because of his old raincoat, messy appearance, half-lit cigar, and deceivingly disorganized manner. We know they're thinking: "Yes, Mr. Columbo, I killed my wife, you scruffy little man, but you'll never catch me." Invariably, at the show's conclusion as the apparently defeated Columbo prepares to depart, declaring how much he admires and respects the perpetrator, he pauses as if a thought just came to mind. And he says, "Oh, by the way, sir..." Every time he mumbles those words, it's the beginning of the end for the killer.

My recommended wording is precise and proven. *Oh, by the way* not only serves as an excellent transition; it also lowers barriers and overcomes initial resistance. A key phrase is *who would appreciate this same level of service* because it infers a high level of service to a high-quality client. The balance of the words ask specifically, but softly and politely in the correct manner, for referrals and tell how to send them.

Learn to ask for referrals. Most people won't think of referring you unless you ask. Use the right words to create the desired responsiveness. There's an entire sequenced dialogue I've developed for this. I call it my *Big 3*, and I've made it an integral part of my conversation with clients:

1. ***Can I be of any help?*** *"Hi, John, this is Brian Buffini calling. How are you? How's the family? And your business? The reason I'm calling is to let you know about my Client Appreciation Program. You're an important part of it. If I can help you in any way, don't hesitate to call...."*

2. *"**I want you to know the value you represent to me as a client.** John, it was a pleasure for me to represent you recently, and I look forward to serving you and your family again. My business depends on working with good people like you and taking care of you, your family, and your friends and associates..."*

3. *"**Oh, by the way,** John, if you know of anyone who is thinking of buying or selling a home who would appreciate this same level of service, just give me a call with their name and number. I'll be happy to follow up with them for you. Does that sound good to you? Great, John! I'll be in touch. Thank you...and take care.*

Every time I'd say "Oh, by the way..." to a client, I was that much closer to getting a referral. The magic words were brief, specific, and acceptable. I started using the phrasing to conclude every call following up an Item of Value. It didn't take long to catch on. In fact, it became very much connected to everything I did, and its use evolved. I had it printed on the bottom of every Item of Value I sent out. I closed every letter with the dialogue as a final paragraph. The "Oh, by the way..." paragraph appeared on all forms of my business correspondence and printed material.

As a marketing device, it created critical mass for me in a short time. You might say that I became as well-known as Kleenex within the San Diego real estate community.

It worked wonderfully well, and it was fun. My clients enjoyed the interplay and really got into it. The more it became established, the more effective it became. Often when I was on the phone with them, before I'd get to say "Oh, by the way...", they'd chuckle and beat me to it: "Oh, by the way, Brian, don't forget to say 'Oh by the way...' ha ha ha". It became almost a game to them and set the climate for marvelous exchanges between us. I was always serving first, and that is important to remember; there is an order in which things should be done. Eventually, after getting used to this system, they'd ask me, "How's business?" That was because they were genuinely interested in how my business was doing. And I would say, "You know what? My business is doing great, but I'm never too busy for any of your referrals. If you ever come across people who are thinking about buying or selling a home, just give me a call with their name and number, and I'll be happy to follow up with them for you."

Give. Ask. Receive.

Judging by the success and referrals these words have generated, I believe that this dialogue could be used effectively by every service business and by every business person seeking leads and referrals. It would only require a simple word change to match the nature of the business: "If you know of anyone who is thinking of buying or selling an automobile...home air-conditioning... bedroom furniture" and so on. It has worked wonders for me and thousands of others.

"Oh, by the way..." has become my signature line and my calling card.

CHAPTER 10

A note can be more than its message

My signature has appeared on many pieces of paper over my years in business. I've signed contracts, letters, legal papers and forms of all description. None is more important than the personal notes I write out by hand and send out every day. **Handwritten personal notes** comprise the next element of my system.

Actually, I continued the practice and emphasized it in my system. The idea came originally from watching an interview with George Bush, Sr. in the late 1980s. The interviewer asked him what was the number one thing he'd done that had gotten him into the White House. His answer was immediate, so immediate that I knew he placed extreme importance on it. The answer was "handwritten personal notes." President Bush said that, every morning at 6:30 AM, in the Oval Office and for years prior to that, his first activity was to sit down and write ten personal notes to people who had come to mind the day before. They were people he wanted to remember or encourage or felt the need to thank. It impressed me that he diligently took the time to do that. It showed his caring nature, good manners and intelligence.

I remember thinking: if it can get him to the White House, maybe it can help me sell a lot of white houses. And I set out to write personal notes every single day. That gave me a greater appreciation of President Bush's stamina and fortitude. It was tough. There were days I felt like writing notes, and there were days I didn't. Sometimes, I was excruciatingly busy. I recall one painful evening in particular. I had sold six homes that day. The average realtor in North America sold between six to seven homes a year, and I had just done that in one day. I was exhausted. It was late, and I was walking out of the office with my briefcase overflowing with contracts. Out of the corner of my eye, I spied the ten unwritten notes for that day. I sighed and sat down and wrote them. And I'm glad I did. I'm going to share with you that, over the course of my career, those notes proved far more valuable than the six transactions I'd done that day. Because they were the beginnings of my adherence to a system.

I made the notes a discipline and emphasized them as a component of my system. During my calls to clients, I was often told family and personal news, and I made that the subject of a note. I sent them to fellow agents, people in supporting businesses, and just plain persons I came in contact with during the week. If someone told me their son was playing in a Little League championship game that weekend, I'd take the time to write a personal note: *Dear John - Hope Billy has a great time at the Little League tournament. It's a good life.*
Brian Buffini.

A note doesn't have to be lengthy. It can be as brief as that. But it does have to be handwritten and pertinent. It's not so much what you say as that you took the time and cared enough to write it yourself. That says much more than the actual message, and it leaves a lasting impression. Neither beauty nor penmanship count for much. It is truly the thought that counts. My penmanship has never been the best. Back in school in Dublin, my teacher, Sister Mary, used to say that my handwriting looked like a spider had dipped its butt in an inkwell and walked across the page.

Even with my scribble, people appreciated that I had taken the time to write them a personal note. It's a nice thing to do and a great way to invest a little bit in someone else. And it will always get read. When we receive our mail, the pieces we all open first are the ones that are personally handwritten.

Every day, I walked into the office and wrote ten personal notes. I put my business card in, addressed the envelope, and put a stamp on it. I'm not saying it was easy to do or that I never missed a day or that I didn't have help. My secretary put ten blank notes and envelopes on my desk every morning. If I didn't write ten notes on Monday (because of a catastrophic natural disaster), Tuesday morning she'd put ten more there; that would make 20. If, God forbid, I didn't write those out (because of a near-death experience), on Wednesday there'd be ten more;

30 notes to catch up with! And it would go on, until there'd be a large mound of notes awaiting my poor penmanship.

Because of my dedication to this task, we had devices in the office to remind me to write the notes: white message boards displayed the number "10" with a big blue star around it; or "50" with a big red star surrounding it. (That's the week of the great floods in San Diego when I couldn't get into the office.) Our technology progressed, and my secretary turned these into screen-savers to remind me. Ten notes a day, five days a week! I joke about it, and I groan about it, but I promise you that nothing in my business career ever took less time, effort or money and produced as big a result.

In my opinion, handwritten personal notes are the greatest catalyst to the compounding effect of the referral system.

I've seen their effectiveness repeatedly in business and their value to the recipients in human terms. To this day, I still stick to the regimen of note-writing. Through Providence Systems, I receive 700 to 800 letters and cards a month. The primary activity every day for my assistant Becky and me is responding with a personal handwritten note to as many as we can.

Thank you, President Bush, for bringing home to me the importance of this personal touch.

At Providence Systems, personal notes and cards have become the mainstay means of written communication for coaches to their clients. In fact, we write so many cards that we are perhaps the only business with a complete Hallmark® shop within our headquarters.

As a postscript to this discussion of personal notes, take time and care with all your correspondence. Every letter is a reflection of your character and competence...and an opportunity to ask for a referral. Systematize. Develop model letters for all purposes and situations: to introduce yourself, to present special events or offers, to endorse someone. As the need for a letter arises, keep the model on your computer and adapt it for similar uses. And remember to ask for referrals with every letter by concluding with the "Oh, by the way...." paragraph.

CHAPTER 11
Pop by

Personal contact is the final major element of the system. Get out and see people face to face. Do it on a regular, systematic basis so you don't allow too much time to pass between visits or miss anyone. Remember, out of sight is out of mind. **The face-to-face visit is still the best way to cement a relationship and build rapport.** It's also the quickest and most effective way to generate referrals while honoring your clients.

When I started in business and went door to door to sell, I didn't really enjoy the experience. I knew that the people whose doors I knocked on didn't usually enjoy it either. So, instead of knocking on strangers' doors for business, I decided to **pop by** and visit the people in my database as friends. Back in Ireland, we consider this an act of friendship, and it is welcomed by people who know each other well; friends frequently pop by to say hello. I adapted this courtesy for my clients.

I found that my pop-bys were welcomed by the "A" people in my database. I'd call them a day or so before to let them know I would be in their area between such and such a time and that I was just going to pop by their office to say Hello. I let them know the visit wouldn't take long or be for any specific reason; I just wanted to drop by and see how they were doing. Invariably, they would be happy to see me.

I made it a point to hold these visits to 15 minutes so that I didn't interrupt their work for too long or wear out my welcome. For my own efficiency, I scheduled my pop-bys in clusters. That way, I could make multiple visits to other clients in the area within a certain time frame. I planned a route and made my pop-bys with dispatch and vigor. I left my car's motor running, and I remained standing during my entire visit. Ah, it's amazing what lengths a gregarious Irishman will go to in order to keep a conversation brief.

During the course of the conversation, I always made sure to ask for a referral. That was accomplished by injecting my Big 3 dialogue:

1. Can I be of any help to you or your business in any way? If I can, don't hesitate to call me.

2. I want to make sure you know how much I value you as a client. I look forward to serving you.

3. Oh, by the way...

I always brought an Item of Value for them and followed up my visit by sending a handwritten personal note.

> Never go visiting with one arm as long as the other.
> — Theresa Buffini, my mother

It's simple courtesy and good manners to bring a gift with you. And it matters to the person you're visiting. That's the main reason why I always brought an Item of Value. My mother taught us to always be carrying a little gift when we went to visit someone.

On every pop-by, I made sure to have it in my hand as I came through the door. Some of our Providence people have developed imaginative items for their pop-bys, such as bringing a bag of microwave popcorn with a label that reads: *Just popping by to say hello.* It's corny, but most effective. You're limited only by your own drive and inventiveness.

On many occasions at training programs across the country, attending realtors have come to me and said, "I have a very wealthy clientele. I can't be popping by with these little piddly items." Let me share with you that it's a misconception. It also shows their misunderstanding of people who have wealth. The top two percent of the wealthiest people in America are five times more likely to use a coupon than people of lesser wealth. Don't underestimate the receptivity of a high-end client to a useful gift, no matter how inexpensive it may be. Don't be afraid to bring those little piddling Items of Value.

When I made it a practice, I found that there was no one who was beyond being affected by a small token of caring and kindness. My father had a marvelous saying for it: "There's a shortage of love and appreciation in the world. If you give it out in slices, it will come back in loaves." I gave it out in little Items of Value, and it came back in respect, referrals, and real estate success.

Make pop-bys a regular part of your business week. Nothing can replace personal contact. Find time and ways to respect and repay your best clients with more of your attention. I often did this by taking my Super A people to lunch or dinner. Arrange a lunch appointment. Sit down and talk and laugh over a good meal and a cup of coffee. And be sure to pick up the bill. Sharing a meal is the most ancient form of hospitality, care and respect. It is equally nourishing to your business.

At Providence events and in our coaching, we encourage members to take other business people to lunch and share these referral concepts. It's an ideal opportunity to talk to them about how to do business by referral. After all, every business person in America needs more and better referrals. The problem is that most people don't know how to generate them pro-actively. Try it out. After reading this book, sit down with a business owner over lunch and discuss doing business by referral. Share the information you've read and give them some tips and examples from this material. You'll find that the people you help with their business will want to help you with yours.

Again, don't be afraid to end the conversation with: "Oh, by the way, if you know of anyone who is thinking of buying or selling a home and would appreciate this same level or service, just give me a call with their name and number, and I'll be happy to follow up with them for you."

> Learn to help people with more than just their jobs; help them with their lives.
> — Jim Rohn

CHAPTER 12
It's alive! It's alive!

Up to now, I've spent the first part of this book telling you how and why my referral system came to be. It took me a lot of time and tinkering to get the components right and to put it all together correctly. And it took me these many pages to tell you about it; that's my Irish heritage; a bit of the blarney goes a long way in telling and selling. Now I'm going to tell you what happened after I put the system to work in my business.

As I first put the system to the test in my business, I felt like Doctor O'Frankenstein. I suffered the same anxieties the fictional doctor must have felt when he raised his creation to the heavens. I felt the same elation when I saw the first stirrings of success. He screamed, "It's alive! It's alive!" over a thunder-and-lightning storm. I told my wife, "It's working! It's working!" over dinner.

Unlike poor Frankenstein, my system worked well right from the start. It was wonderfully reassuring to know that I hadn't created a monster. The system generated referrals rapidly, and they were the right kind of referrals, the people and quality I was after. It didn't take long for me to be certain I had made the right choice in deciding to work exclusively by referral. My clients caught on quickly and truly enjoyed being part of the process. The response from my "A" and "A+" clients went far beyond my expectations, and it kept going and growing. My business boomed and kept booming. At the end of the first year, I had more than doubled my sales and tripled my net income. I had to increase the size of my staff to handle the contact demands and the paperwork this created. And I had to add associates and train them to use my system. Six months later, I was using trained people on a team basis to handle the referrals and transactions.

The growth demands went with the territory, and I was happy to handle them. I was well on my way to becoming a member of the Million Dollar Club. Not the Million Dollar Sales Club, but the Million in the Bank society! Time and success have dimmed my memories of any bad occasions, glitches or minor failures in those years, but there were some. Since I never dwell on negatives, I'll simply say that I learned from them and progressed; again, that goes with the territory. I constantly worked to refine and improve the system and elements as I went. That's an ongoing part of the process for me to this day.

I don't wish to make too much of my own success. My experience is described here in general terms only to verify the effectiveness of the system. And to inspire you to consider working exclusively by referral yourself. Put it this way: my personal results validated my system, its unique methods and practices, and the thinking that went into it.

It proved to me that the concepts of commitment and service were correct; the precepts of client selectivity and personalized attention were right; and the elements - Client Appreciation Program, Items of Value, personal handwritten notes, pop-bys, and Oh, by the way dialogue - all truly worked together in sequenced combination to produce referrals, as I had hoped. It also verified my beliefs that people have a built-in eagerness to refer exceptional service to others, that focusing on the preferred few pays off, and that the best sources of referrals can be found among the clients you already have.

Perhaps the most satisfying thing success proved to me was that my pro-active system offered a better alternative than the sad collection of passive traditional sales methods I'd tried and found lacking.

I eventually got to the point where I had more business than I ever thought I'd have. In fact, I had all the business that I wanted. While the financial security and personal trappings of success were gratifying and enjoyable, those things weren't the best part. The most rewarding part was the people I was serving. You know how they say that true success in business is enjoying what you do? Well, I really enjoyed my clients and the entire process of serving them.

> **If you share a good idea long enough, it will eventually fall on good people.** — Jim Rohn

For their part, they couldn't do enough to send me referrals. They enjoyed being the cause of my success. That's because they were getting my extra-best and they were overflowing to tell their friends about that extra-best. The guru of the motivational industry, Ken Blanchard, wrote the book, *Raving Fans*, which discusses this very thing - people who are not just your customers, but your raving fans as well. My system created a situation like that for me. I got to experience the privilege and joy of their enthusiasm in my business.

There were other significant benefits that came from the system at work, beyond anything material. These benefits improved virtually every area of my life: not only business and financial, but personal, family and spiritual as well. Most importantly, it transformed me...to want to share my success with others. This is not to suggest I'm the Finished Product; I still have a long way to go.

Simply put, I became a better person because of this system, and that's no blarney. I make a point of telling this to all who attend my training sessions across the country. I say that there are four stages of growth, and we go through them like a caterpillar turning into a butterfly. We start out working to survive...until we gain stability...allowing us to achieve success...which gives us significance. Survival, stability, success, significance. Am I right? That's the way the system took me.

It will take you from a position of uncertainty and fear about your next lead to confident predictability for the number and quality of leads you'll generate. After consistently monitoring and measuring my business, I eventually got to the point where I knew within a certain range how many referrals would come in each month. It wasn't a bang-bang situation of instant response. I found that many referrals are developed over a period of time and may be caused months ahead. I'm reminded of the old joke about babies: the first one comes anytime; the rest take at least nine months each. I've received referrals that were sparked by Items of Value I sent out a year before, sometimes two or three years before! By studying the specific cause and effect of each referral, I came to know statistically how people would respond to the system monthly.

Here's another thing I learned by monitoring and measuring the effectiveness of my system: it caused referrals to come in whether the market was good, bad or indifferent. That's the beauty of it! Despite the current state of your market, referrals will always happen. My business grew consistent and predictable. That stability gave me peace of mind, knowing I could fully serve my clients, the referrals would be there, and my future was secure.

You've probably met people in sales who believe that every month is a new month for business or that every year is a new year for sales. I know people with twenty years in real estate who actually have only one year's worth of experience repeated twenty times. They start from zero every year. By that, I mean there is no continuation or carry-over in their business from year to year. It evidences a lack of long-term thinking and a faulty approach. That's not a belief I share. Because of a particular feature of my system, I don't have to think that way.

The most awesome benefit of this referral system is **the compounding effect** it has on your business. I saw it happen for me and subsequently for thousands I've trained through Providence Systems. And I continue to be astonished at the growth it produces.

The compounding effect works simply and consistently over time, similar to the way 12% compound interest works to turn $100 invested monthly into more than $1,180,000 at the end of 40 years. Once you get a referral from an individual, and it goes well, the person referred becomes your advocate as well as your client. That advocate/client refers you to many others over time, and they become your advocates. The more advocates you have, the more your business grows.

The more the business grows, the more client/advocates you gain, the more the business grows. It's like ivy, self-propagating and spreading.

Each and every month, each and every year, my business got stronger and stronger and grew and grew and grew. No, I hadn't expected it to grow exponentially, as it did. Yes, it was the result of working at it and having good fortune. But more than that, it was because of the soundness of the system and the concepts it was based on. The compounding effect is built in. It stems from proactive use of the simple, practical elements in proper combination and sequence. I would comment that the personal handwritten notes and the Items of Value have a noticeable catalytic value in this. They seem to contain a growth hormone. A single element may ultimately result in three or four referrals, or more over time.

After a while, I went to my office every morning, knowing I would receive referrals during the day. Eventually, there was never a day that I didn't get referrals. Using the system, I had caused them to happen. Pro-actively! And they were the best clients to serve...full service, full fee...and I genuinely liked them. If I had to cold-call to make a living, I'd have failed because I hated doing it.

But I never had a problem calling people who'd be happy to hear from me. I never got an upset stomach driving to a pop-by with an Item of Value for someone who'd be glad to see me. I enjoyed what I was doing, and I built a business that gave a great return for the investment of my time and effort. This is how I built my fortune.

CHAPTER 13

Believe in Providence

I believe in divine guidance. Things do generally happen for the best. What we do in life and our very natures are part of a master plan. Our actions, our achievements and failures, are inspired by a force larger than ourselves. Call it providence.

Now, I have been extraordinarily blessed, and I am appropriately thankful. But it took me a while to properly acknowledge the gift I'd been given. I'd found a slot machine that paid a continuing jackpot, and I was enjoying the heck out of it. For a while, I reveled in my success, glad it was good for everyone close to me, convinced it was the result of my own ingenious gifts. However, after a while, I found that I enjoyed helping other people become successful more than any of my own accomplishments.

The system seemed to have the potential to generate enough for everybody, so I explained it to a few realtors I knew could use it. They tried it, and it worked for them. And they liked it so much that they kept it pretty much to themselves. But a funny thing happened on their way to their safe-deposit boxes. The benefits of the system spilled over and, more often than not, flowed back to me. I gradually noticed that I was receiving referrals through those agents. The referrals came when one of their clients was looking for a home in my area. I noticed that they were good referrals and quality people. I reciprocated, and it grew. Just what I needed...more business! The clients I sent to them referred me to others who were looking in my area. Word spread, and a few more realtors asked me about my referral system.

The more I did of this, the more return I got from it. It grew into a phenomenon. My dad was right...again. The loaves were comin' in hot and fast. Give to givers, and they'll give back more. I noticed, and an idea began to take shape in my mind. There was no moment of Epiphany, no ray of heavenly light; just a slow, gradual realization that others could benefit from my business discovery and I should share it.

I did some more heavy thinking about sharing and some research about applying it to referral systems. Since I am a God-respecting man, that took me to the Good Book. I found direct references there. I refined these into a set of principles that I relay to those I train today. I call these *The Seven Biblical Principles of the Referral Process*, presented here in excerpted form:

1. Why does the referral system work?
For whatever a man sows this he will also reap...And let us not lose heart in doing good. For in due time we shall

reap if we do not grow weary. So then, while we have opportunity, let us do good to all men.

—Galatians

2. How should we serve clients?
Do nothing from selfish or empty conceit, but with humility of mind let each of you regard one another as more important than himself. Do not merely look out for your own interests, but also for the interest of others.

—Philippians

3. How should we plan?
Commit your works to the Lord and your plans will be established...The mind of man plans his way but the Lord directs his steps...Trust in the Lord with all your heart and do not lean on your own understanding.

—Proverbs

4. How should we work?
Whatever you do, work at it with all your heart

—Colossians

5. How should we use the gifts we have been given?
For to those who use well what they are given, even more shall be given and they shall have an abundance; but from those who do not use well what they are given, even what little they have will be taken away.

—Matthew

6. How should we fulfill our potential and grow?
Do not be conformed to this world, but be transformed by the renewing of your mind.   —Romans

7. What is the the ultimate goal of our work, our business, and our lives?
Let your light shine before men in such a way that they may see your good work. —Matthew

This scriptural validation confirmed my thinking and guided my subsequent actions...along with a shove in the right direction, again from my wife.

Around that time, to polish my public-speaking skills, I joined a program to talk about the real estate business. I chose to speak about referrals, and Beverly came to hear me. That night, she said to me, "Brian, you're not doing what you were meant to do. You have a gift for public speaking, and you should be using it. You should be a speaker because you can do it so well, training and entertaining people at the same time."

As I mentioned previously, Bev believes I'm entitled to her opinions, and I value them. Listening equates to being interested; hearing is often just waiting for someone to be done talking; I always listen to my wife. Enough said. That was all I needed to hear.

To make a long story short, I shifted my role in the real estate business...from using the referral system to teaching and training others to utilize the system. With Bev's concurrence and with the advice and assistance of some people close to me, I started up a small seminar company. Its mission was to spread the word about my system to real estate professionals. Another leap of faith. More planning, structuring and systematizing. More humble beginnings and hard work. But with a higher purpose this time. One of the first things to do was decide on a name. I called it *Providence*.

We established Providence Seminars behind the Post Office in Vista, California in 1996. I say "we" because I couldn't possibly have done it alone. Beverly and my brothers, John and Gary, were instrumental in helping me get started. They did the hard work while I lined up contacts and contracts, potential clients, and speaking engagements. A wonderful woman and close friend, Cynthia McKim, put together a small staff of coaches and support people and supervised them. Her husband Patrick handled the books and billing. Together, we all multi-tasked and developed operating procedures, approaches, curricula, media and promotional materials, seminar agendas, manuals, everything necessary, most of it from scratch. Under Cynthia's leadership, the cadre of coaches created and refined coaching and calling procedures. Everyone contributed importantly. It was a wonderful time of working together.

The fledgling business flew. We refined, improved and corrected, and it grew. We gained clients and coaches and staff and moved to larger offices. The seminar events became larger and better, more professional and polished. Providence proved the merit of the referral system with increasing popularity to an ever-widening audience. We gained members all across America, from California to Connecticut.

Along the way, we had our share of mishaps, snafus, and misadventures - everything from misplaced desks and malfunctioning sound equipment to office fires, broken waterpipes and hurt feelings. But that, too, has passed away. Now, instead of herding myself and a few weary assistants onto fatiguing commercial flights to put on a program, we fly directly to cities around the country in Providence's private jet. That is one trapping of success I permit myself to thoroughly enjoy. Only someone who has traveled as much as I have can fully appreciate the humanizing convenience of it.

All the effort has paid off again, better this time because our programs and coaching are improving more and more people's businesses and lives.

Providence continues to grow. Now named Providence Systems, it has become the largest personal coaching company in the country. A staff of well over one hundred is headquartered in an ultra-modern office complex in Carlsbad, California. More than 600,000 business professionals have been trained through our seminars; thousands are in the coaching program, individually mentored by their own coach, selected from over 100 people who have received special training for this job. Thousands more have been informed, trained and entertained at our Turning Point Retreats, two-day events held each month in major U.S. cities.

Upwards of 5,000 enthusiastic members attend our year-end Mastermind Summit program to celebrate their and our success each December. These gala events are held in fun locations like Las Vegas and San Diego and feature outstanding speakers - astronaut Neil Armstrong in 2002 and business philosopher Jim Rohn in 2001. You might say we're doing all right, getting the message out.

> **Through our seminars, we've trained over 600,000 business professionals. I like to believe we've helped to make their lives better as well.**
> — Cynthia McKim, Providence Systems

I look at Providence now and almost can't believe how large and sophisticated it's become! The thousands we coach on a bi-weekly basis, the thousands of personal success stories from enthusiastic members, the capacity audiences at our events, the many lives we've helped to make better - all of these things demonstrate the great effects of the system, our programs and the coaching. As you consider all this, keep in mind that Providence sells itself. Membership, enrollment in coaching, attendance at events...all happen by referral.

Providence operates exclusively by referral. We practice what we preach.

Here's a quick summary of what we do: Providence provides the systems for individuals and organizations to:

1. Generate leads in business through building relationships.
2. Prioritize time and activities to maintain lifestyle, balance and achieve maximum profit.
3. Make disciplined, informed business choices and financial decisions.
4. Identify and manage the inherent personal abilities and gifts people are uniquely born to use.

What is the basis for Providence's programs and coaching? Essentially, it's all based on the philosophies, approaches and system elements I told you about earlier. It is important to note that these programs and precepts have been amplified and perfected at Providence. As one member from Massachusetts put it, "Ya got maw and bettah." I agree, we keep giving more and better.

We now deal more specifically with related business and personal issues: running your own business like a business; managing your time and priorities to fullest advantage; handling and tracking finances; setting and achieving vibrant, realistic goals; improving profitability; knowing yourself and your abilities; and much more.

These and a wide range of self-management and self-improvement subjects are constantly developed and added to our core programs. The reason for them is to help our members in every way we can. The need to include them arose from each issue's obvious importance and relevance to our members. Each started as a generalized request for advice or help from our subscribers. The bottom line is that we respond to their needs and offer sound guidance for almost every aspect of business and personal improvement.

How do we do all this? By live events and learning systems designed to focus participants on achieving their goals. And by training and coaching members through a system-oriented approach to their goals. Why does it work so well? Personalized coaching by Providence professionals ties it all together and causes it to work.

If you're a professional salesperson or simply an interested business person, you owe it to yourself to take a look at ways to meet your goals and to improve. Everything we do is designed and personalized to help individuals in their quest to better themselves. Providence provides the training and coaching to help you achieve a better business and a better life, believe me.

I'm proud of what my original ideas have become. I enjoy every day with the people of Providence. It's a good life!

On a personal note, it gives me the opportunity to work closely with my family. My oldest brother, Gary, is Director of Sales at Providence. His secondary job is keeping me humble. My older brother, John, heads up our ability management program, which he conceived and developed. John is a leading expert on personal profiling and the leading educator on ability management. His book, *Be Yourself,* is acknowledged as the definitive work on the subject. My younger brother, Dermot, is the manager for Providence events and sergeant-at-arms. My youngest brother, Kevin, is a mainstay in our Abilities Management Division and has been instrumental in the growth of Providence. Beverly buzzes in when I need her advice or assistance, operating in the capacity of Queen Bee, a position she's earned by her savvy and industry.

While it is not family-operated, strictly speaking, Providence does carry on the sense of that tradition in caring service and responsiveness. The entire Providence membership and staff have grown to regard us as the *The*

Buffinis, a family that works wonderfully well together. Many have told us that our closeness as a family and cohesiveness as a working unit are rewarding to see; some say inspiring to them personally. I know that for me the rapport and reliability of working with my family have been a joy and a blessing. They're my kind of people.

CHAPTER 14
Talk to the coach

Have you ever bought exercise equipment and not used it? Have you ever had a great idea and not done anything about it? Have you ever gone to a terrific seminar and come home all fired up for action? And then let that energy and commitment fizzle through inaction? Those failures demonstrate the need and reason to be coached. It's difficult to improve yourself by yourself.

> Nothing great was ever achieved without somebody helping.
> — Althea Gibson

That's why personal trainers have become so popular with millions who are into physical fitness. It's the reason great athletic coaches are revered by players and fans. That's because great coaches have the ability to instill winning spirit and have developed the systems and methods necessary to draw the best out of you.

Everyone wants to win, and that may mean overcoming our own failings and our own bad habits. We all want to be shown how to succeed and learn the best way to go about it. Coaching provides that expertise and application.

For the same reason, job and business coaching is now recognized as essential in the commercial world. This is a relatively recent development in business, a trend of the 1980s that keeps gaining momentum. It grew out of the corporate emphasis on employee training and the focus of excellence-in-management programs.

I learned the importance of good coaching in school and by participating in team sports. I came to value great coaching all the more when I saw the lifetime effect it had on Beverly. Apart from sports, I saw the value of it in education, skills acquisition, and training for the arts. Good students learned from good teachers. Good teachers invariably were good coaches. I watched personal coaching grow from a trendy fitness activity to a staple of improved job performance. And, from the beginning, I put coaching into the game plan as the central capability at Providence. It is "the straw that stirs the drink." No doubt about it.

So, as we train business professionals, we coach them to personal success. One on one in a win-win situation. I view it as supremely important to achievement and success for just about everybody. **Personal coaching provides the structure and support we all need.** The number-one golfer in the world relies on constant coaching to stay on top of his game. Jack Nicklaus, Tiger Woods and Michael Jordan all credit much of their success to their coaches. I'm convinced that each of us is better served by that kind of help and discipline for our business and life.

Coaching is at the heart of Providence success, and I have good reason to be glad I emphasized its importance. Early on, some of our members...intelligent, motivated, tough-minded people...thought that the coaching was unnecessary for them to reach the next level in their business and life. The principles and practices were clear to them, and they opted to do it by themselves. On their own, they tried to apply the principles of my referral system to their businesses. Some did amazingly well, but many of the do-it-yourselfers achieved considerable frustration, and they let me know about it. They shared the same problems in common: no accountability; not knowing all the steps to properly utilize the system; not being sure of the sequence; being nagged by nay-sayers; fighting the traditional practices and philosophies of the business; inability to master the dialogues and nuances of the system; and so on and so on.

The fooler is that the system seems so simple. It's clear, concise and practical, and it seems sensible and easy. And it is! But there's a lot more to it than meets the eye. Taking in the flow of information from a single Turning Point Retreat is like getting hit full-force by a gushing fire hose. It usually takes attendees several events to cover and digest all that information. It helps immensely to be coached by someone who knows the system and understands your business. Our coaches get to know their charges personally and are trained to guide them through the individual problems and pitfalls.

I tell all my audiences: "It's not an easy thing to do. Consider the coaching. Talk to a coach." And I explain what a Providence ClubNet coach can do with a member: Establish goals and create action steps to make them happen. Focus on accountability. Provide empathy, encouragement and championing. Celebrate achievements, and set new goals. That's quite a bit, wouldn't you say? That's what we do.

This Step-by-Step program matches the coaching client with a skilled personal trainer who is well-versed in the system and knows how to make it work. It's not scripted or "canned"; it's responsive to the personal goals of the individual being coached. Member and coach get together by phone twice a month.

First, we help you identify your strengths and abilities. Then, you and your coach establish realistic goals tailored to your needs and wants. Together, you create a step-by-step plan to achieve optimum, balanced results in your business and in your life. Over the course of this program, the coach provides ongoing support to help you reach and exceed your goals. It's like regular exercise: you need it, and it's good for you. The average ClubNet member experiences a 70% increase in net income and a 100% increase in time off.

> Our coaches help you identify obstacles and create your own unique solutions for them.
> — Cynthia McKim

What makes our coaching so effective? At Providence, we developed the process to assure quality control and continual improvement. Lead coaches provide third-party accountability and support for each coach-and-client pairing. All our coaches receive extensive, special training to make sure that clients receive full value from their coaching relationship. With more than 100 trained, experienced coaches, we can customize the coaching relationship like no one else.

> This program has been extremely helpful in guiding me through my plan and keeping me on track. It has given me insights that have allowed me to be more effective in my role. I highly recommend personal coaching as an avenue for accomplishing more and obtaining better results.
> — Avram Goldman, President
> COO, Coldwell Banker, Northern California

As a feature of this program, I conduct a live (and lively) monthly conference call for all ClubNet members. The format is open forum with call-ins after our topic of the month or guest interview. It gives me a great way to put in my two-cents worth...and stay in touch and in tune with everyone.

The Coaching Diamond

Here's how our coaching system is organized to deliver one-on-one personalized attention with total support from the entire Providence Coaching Division.

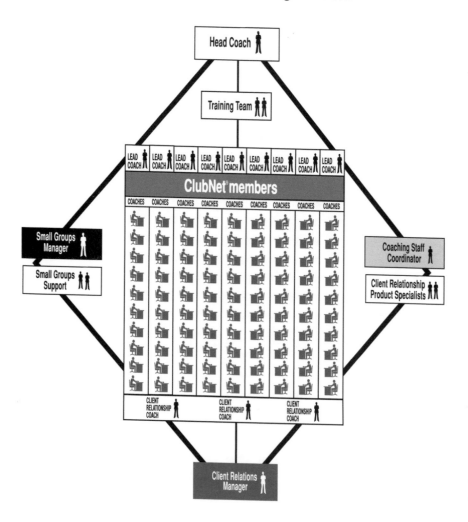

Accountability makes Providence coaching effective. It gives clients a person who knows and cares about them and their business and tracks their achievement. The coach is both a facilitator and a means of measuring progress. Accountability enhances short and long-term goal achievement, time management, and database management. It is vital to ongoing training because it registers the learning pace for the referral dialogues and gauges implementation stages of the referral system elements. It tracks success by monthly reporting on profit-and-loss, client activity, number of referrals, closings, pop-bys, personal notes, and other important statistics. It is the coach's tool to keep you on track.

> As a brand new agent, I attended Brian's two-day program and decided to run my business strictly by referral, virtually from day one. In the next 11 months with the support of my coach, I closed 49 transactions. This system works...and I'm sticking with it. — Sue West, Realty Executives, Tempe, Arizona

Championing is an exceptional aspect of our coaching. It describes perfectly the quality of being there for another person in a combination of roles: supporter, guardian, motivator, promoter, and encourager. It's a word we used in Ireland to mean standing up for another person, acting in their best interest. Perhaps because of my heritage, I favor the word for its Old-World roots in knighthood and chivalry.

It comes from the medieval practice of a knight acting as a champion, protecting and defending those who came under his care...with chivalry, courtesy, and responsibility. Championing is what I train and urge our coaches to deliver.

Mentoring is the other exceptional quality you receive from coaching at the personal level. You deserve a knowledgeable, wise advisor with your best interests at heart. In Greek mythology, Mentor was the loyal friend and wise advisor of Ulysses, and the teacher and guardian of Ulysses' son. So you see, the qualities and need for coaching go back a long, long way.

> **My mentor said, "Let's go do it," not "You go do it."**
> **How powerful when someone says "Let's!"** — Jim Rohn

In my own life, I have been fortunate to have great coaching with championing from wonderful mentors. Foremost are my parents. My mother encouraged us to always do the right thing, to be our own person, and to be all that we could be. Whenever we whined or complained, she had a stock answer. "Get down off that cross, Brian." I can hear her saying now, "We need the wood." My father has always been my champion and mentor and role model. In his quiet, private way, he would take us aside to discuss our individual problems, stay at the dinner table to offer group counseling, advise and lead us through example and hard work.

My older brothers and sister were a great influence for me. Teachers, athletic coaches, friends of the family...great people have been there for me at every stage of my development as a person. They taught me well and pointed me in the right direction.

Since coming to America and entering business, I have been coached, mentored, and championed by some outstanding people.

In particular, renowned business philosopher, Jim Rohn, has had the greatest influence on me with regard to personal growth. He has been mentor, friend and associate. His philosophies and advice on life improvement, motivation and success in business have been invaluable. Another of my mentors is the great Zig Ziglar, the dean of personal-improvement motivators. His wisdom, guidance, and example have inspired and supported me throughout my career. Their thoughts and advice appear in quotes sprinkled throughout this book because they have been of such value to me.

Just think what you can become in business and how your life can be better with a great coach to help you. Coaching is at the heart of it. It is the engine that drives and brings together all the rest.

CHAPTER 15

Personal betterment: a bonus of the system

While the system is designed as a better way to do business, it also has a significant impact for betterment on your personal life. This first became apparent to me when I put the system to work in my real estate office. As I watched every aspect of my business life improve, I became aware that virtually every area of my personal life benefited as well.

The system did improve every aspect of my business life in terms of enjoyment, efficiency, profitability, scheduling and use of time, but it did so much more! It brought me financial security and gave me discipline and direction. Primarily, it gave me peace of mind. That in turn gave me the confidence and conviction to do things correctly and well.

The principles and disciplines of the system carried over to my personal and family relationships, my personal finances and budgeting, my physical and mental well-being, and my spiritual needs. As it developed, it gave me more time to spend with my family, the most important concern and most cherished thing in my life. It permitted me to spend more quality time with my children and Beverly, to participate fully in the kids' growing-up, and to do more with them as a family. It created more time for me to share with my mother and father, sister and brothers. It gave me the means to improve things for all of them, especially my mom and dad, and generally to help friends and others who needed help. It afforded me the time and space for leisure and vacations, to renew myself, which we all need on a regular basis; for reasonable workdays and work-weeks, to pace myself intelligently; and for personal fitness, to maintain my health and energy. It gave me time for formal worship at church, for proper contemplation of spiritual matters, and for participation in worthwhile activities and causes. As much as the time, it left me feeling renewed from my work, with the energy to do all these things.

Sharing the system with others returned much more to me than I gave out. My total life became magnitudes better because of the brightened environment, peace of mind, and joy of being constantly in the company of people I truly liked, cared for, and enjoyed. As I progressed in my career, I tried to analyze this uplift in my life. What I found is that the best way to grow your business, your finances, and all areas of your life is to **gain control and grow yourself**.

As I've already stated, there are four stages of growth. The movement you want is from Survival to Stability to Success to Significance in the five key areas of life: family, financial, career/business, health, and spiritual. To do that, you have to make the commitment to grow and better yourself. That entails facing your deep-seated fears. It also means dispositioning anyone or anything that controls you or causes anger in you. You may have to deal with negative influences in the form of: parents, teachers, friends and associates, environment, trauma, failure, and other factors. You have to do it because avoidance of the negative influences in your life is really the worst thing, isn't it? To grow and get better, you must heal the past. Become a serial optimist. Move on...with the emphasis on move.

> Bless your past for the best that has happened and forget the rest.

You will find that all of this affects you for the better physically as well as mentally. There is an energy from it that propels you to do things with drive and conviction. This brief Buffini Brothers story illustrates the point.

As we made our way through early middle age, my brother John and I put on a few pounds. Dermot and Kevin were young and active enough that weight was not a problem for them. John had a sweet tooth, and his body retained ice cream. We decided to get control of ourselves and our health. Personal trainers, strict exercise regimens, intelligent diets and controlled eating habits - we worked at it to make our bodies fit our advice to clients. John, never athletic, became the buff brother and was delighted. I lost a lot of pounds and was happy to feel and look better.

Now, I'm known in the family as the one who lights the fire and stirs the pot. And I'm a refiner. We were all in such fine physical shape that I thought of a way to improve on our condition. I talked my brothers into entering the San Diego Marathon as a family unit; and I urged them into training for it with me. I wanted all of us to finish the grueling 26 miles. It would be a triumph for the Buffini brothers and an inspiration for all who knew us, I told them. We trained and we ran. We ran and we trained...right up to the week of the marathon.

As we tapered our training, I was proud of them and myself, confident we'd finish with ease. Then, at the last moment, disaster struck. Running when I should have rested, I pulled a hamstring muscle. Pain prevented participation. After all that training, I had to drop out of the race.

Needless to say, they all ran and finished well, John gloriously. And of course, they all needled me unmercifully. I was accused of setting them up, faking an injury, letting the family down. I'm still known as "Marathon Man" to this day, but the stigma is worth it. We all got in great shape; the training provided a basis for all of us to continue working out; I felt great pride in having originated the idea; and our pants all fit.

We had a unified goal, and they achieved it. That's another point we stress at Providence. Set vibrant, realistic personal goals and work to achieve them. Write your goals down; it will articulate and facilitate accomplishment. Expand your comfort zone, as we did through daily training, by affirmation and association with positive people headed in the same direction you are. Give yourself a finish line that tests and stretches your abilities.

This experience illustrates the unexpected outcome of a goal. We may miss in one respect, but still hit an entirely unforeseen benefit. While the joke was on me, my idea greatly benefited my brothers and brought great amusement to many. Mission accomplished.

Having the time to train and get in shape was a result of working within the system. That time would have been unimaginable early in my real estate career. I learned to manage my time, prioritize, and use my time to optimum benefit. You can, too. Time management is part of our training and coaching at Providence. Everyone regards time and moves through time differently. We help you realize your own clock and use it to best advantage.

Looking back now, I realize that a large part of my satisfaction and happiness stems from using my God-given abilities to the fullest. That is an insight I can share with you. Everyone is born with inherent gifts and has abilities that are particular to themselves.

Through our Ability Management program and coaching at Providence, we enable you to identify and manage the inherent personal abilities and gifts you are uniquely born to use. By using a profiling process of interview and analysis, we help people identify and understand their inherent abilities and themselves at a core level. This program empowers them to become the best version of themselves possible, by acting on that awareness. From it, they learn how to leverage their unique abilities personally and professionally. Everyone should do this program. It's a real eye-opener.

All the benefits of the system affect you personally to be all that you can be. That is our over-all goal and the aim of every one of our programs. At our Mastermind Summit each year, we dedicate the time to personal growth and achievement. It is something to be celebrated.

The 5 Key Areas of Life

spiritual

personal mental physical

family & friends

financial

business

CHAPTER 16

The value of values

My strongest encouragement to you is the continuing improvement that the referral system will bring to your life and business. On top of that, it creates a great environment for everything you do. Thousands of success stories and verifiable case studies back this up.

I want you to come away from these pages with the understanding that, not only is this an ideal way to conduct business and live, **it is the most profitable and optimal way to run a business. The built-in success of the system turns on a golden principle, serving my clients to the deepest of their needs, not to the deepest of mine**. The abundance of business comes as a natural result of totally applying that principle.

Many companies and small businesses in America consistently put their self-serving needs first, constantly making decisions based on their short-term return in dollars and cents, only to end up penny-wise and pound-foolish. I regard that as remarkably short-sighted and unbelievably pig-headed.

I've learned an underlying lesson from my career, and I want to share it with you: **Build your business by and to your own values.** It is crucial to your success and happiness. Holding true to yourself and your values will make you passionate and keep you enthused about your work. Your clients will connect with your values. The clients you want will come because your values will coincide with their own. But you must demonstrate your values in some tangible way so your clients will realize them. It won't work with a slogan that announces, "Come and do business with me. You can trust me." Lip service isn't enough. You have to show them your values. And those values have to make a significant difference from the service your competitors provide. You have to give clients that significant difference in whole-hearted service.

Here's a great example: Earlier on, I described my unhappy experience buying a new car. At another time and another dealership, I helped my brother Kevin buy a car, and the experience was beautiful. The same person owned two dealerships; call them Good and Bad. We walked into Good and looked around. They left us alone. When it was apparent that we wanted to talk, someone came over. We had an intelligent conversation with the salesman. He listened intently to what we were looking for, asked our price range and what type of vehicle we wanted, and guided us to those vehicles. We test-drove several cars. When we sat at his desk, he brought coffee and cookies and made us feel comfortable. He explained the dealership's selling procedure and told us the details. There was little discussion; we simply told him what we wanted, and he straightforwardly told us what they needed. That brought us quickly to a meeting of the minds. Their financial person was equally professional and treated us with the same level of care and courtesy. It was a pleasure to buy an automobile from that dealership. Within 30 days, I referred two people to them, and both bought cars from that dealership.

Two months later, I went to dealership Bad with my wife to buy a suburban. Although both dealerships were owned by the same person, the process was aggravatingly different. At Bad, they didn't listen to a word we said and didn't ask us any questions. As we looked at a particular car, they hurried us, "Well, are you ready to buy this one?" Of course we didn't know. We were just trying to determine which was the best vehicle for us, but that didn't seem to matter to them.

"Are you ready to buy this one?! Ready to buy that one?" The Bad people brought over coffee and cookies, but they didn't make us feel comfortable...or even acknowledged. They didn't tell us how the sale would work. We spent unpleasant hours thrashing in negotiation. Bad impression from Bad salespeople! Eventually, Bev had enough and left me to finish up alone. It was my fault that I had assumed the same treatment from twin dealerships. "Let me know if we're buying a car here!" she said loudly as she went out the door.

Because I'm Celtic-stubborn, I finally did get a deal put together. Once we got to the finance person, he was cut from the same cloth, just as miserable to deal with as the rest. The car we bought is fantastic, and I'd recommend it to anyone looking for that sort of suburban. But... under the most painful torture...I wouldn't recommend that dealership. The entire process was ugly. What made it incredible is that the same person owned both dealerships, Good and Bad, but the values and approaches were so different. Good was great in all respects, and our values meshed. Bad gave us a hard time with their philosophy of "find 'em and grind 'em, get 'em in, get 'em out, get 'em sold." Their values put us off.

The differences in values between the two dealerships are apparent in other ways, too. Good spends almost no money on advertising while Bad constantly runs expensive ads, pays pro athletes to promote the dealership, and holds many promotional events. They spend a ton of money on attracting customers without realizing the lifetime value of the customer standing in front of them.

At the Good dealership, there was room for improvement. They let communication, contact, and interest slide. We were obviously eager to give them referrals immediately after the sale, but lack of interest returns lack of interest. If the Good dealership had stayed in touch, sent us little Items of Value or something as reminders, actually asked for referrals, and registered any long-term interest in us as client/customers, we'd have been glad to comply. If I had heard an occasional "Hey, just let me know if you have any friends who want this same kind of service...", I'd gladly have sent them referrals as often as they sent me reminders. And that's what it's all about.

Put in place values that are in harmony with your own belief systems. Work that way, no matter how small or big your organization is. Every person in your organization must hold these values in common, effectively present these values in their own way, and share the same view of how to serve clients. The purpose of this commonality is to achieve consistency in approach by all members of your organization. It also creates a full appreciation of service from your clients. It distinguishes the Good businesses from the Bad.

I've seen this adherence to values work, not just in my career, but in Providence as well. And it works for the thousands of business professionals Providence Systems trains and coaches. We train 50,000 to 60,000 people a year. We coach thousands every month on the in-depth aspects of doing business by referral. In everything we do, we stress the importance of sticking to personal values.

> It is my observation that working to personal values, caring for clients and personal coaching are equally the engines that propel Providence clients to success.
>
> — Tom Gay, CEO of Providence Systems, Inc.

It boils down to "Do to others as you would have others do to you." Sound familiar? I didn't invent it. It's been the best advice since The Sermon on the Mount. Make a significant commitment to the values and principles you believe in. Observing these values, serve your clients to the deepest of their needs. Then share with them that you'd appreciate their help to similarly serve anyone else they know. Give them an opportunity to reciprocate. Teach them how to refer, and they will send you one referral after another. Next thing you know, you'll have a business that is built on this process. Every time you say, "Oh, by the way...," it will result in a referral that benefits everyone involved.

Let's put some real numbers to the points I've made. For the first 4,000 people we've had come through our coaching program, the average increase in net income in the first year has been 70%. While this high percentage is a reflection of how well we coach our clients, it also shows the power of the referral process itself. And this high level of success does not apply only to individuals who own small businesses; we've seen the same percentages in larger companies and corporations utilizing our referral system and coaching.

One of the best examples is Home Savings of America, a well-known bank and mortgage company on the West Coast. They had been among the sponsors for certain of our training events. Attending these seminars and listening to our curriculum gave them the idea to apply our system to their industry.

We put in place a program by which we initially trained some of their salespeople, then coached key individuals. Within their corporation, they produced a client appreciation program and named it *Best Regards*. They started sending out Items of Value to thousands of clients every month. This was an innovative move for a bank, unique in their industry. They sent out change-of-address labels to their clients when they closed a mortgage. At the holiday season, they sent out gift tags for clients to mark presents. Every month, they printed up helpful hints and tips that went out to their preferred clients.

In just one year, their return was staggering. They went from 17 million dollars in retail loans a day to 63 million! Their cost to generate a lead fell from $157 to $17 per lead. Eventually, we trained more than 500 of their salespeople in these systems. The results were spectacular.

It is my rock-solid belief that applying your personal values to your business will translate into tremendous financial value in return. What goes around comes around.

CHAPTER 17

End by getting started

A lot of people will read this book and say, "Wow, it would be really nice to operate a business like that! What a dream it would be to do things to my own standards..work only with great people that I choose...know that I can serve them well...trust that they'll refer other good people to me for business...and have it all work just the way this Buffini guy says it will."

They'll turn it over in their minds and think: "Nah, it sounds too good to be true. Real estate is too tough. It's a dog-eat-dog business. Kill or be killed. Nice guys finish last. There's no way this referral system can work. It's a nice concept, a good idea, but it's probably pie in the sky. I'm not buying it."

My answer is, "Believe it." I believe in it because I've lived it, watched it work, and want to share it with people for all the right reasons. Learn more about Providence and me. Go to the website at **www.providencesystems.com** and find out more. Better still, come to a Turning Point Retreat when one is scheduled near you. If you're not convinced by a day or two with me, I believe you will be by the Providence members in the audience. They use the system and are always eager to share their success stories with doubting newcomers. And keep in mind that the thousands of Providence subscribers are living proof of the system's credibility.

Welcome the opportunity to change your life for the better. Get started. Don't let a good idea get away. Try it yourself. Use what you've learned from this book.

> You don't have to be great to start, but you do have to start to be great. — Zig Ziglar

Here's a brief review of the process and some points of advice to help you get started in putting the system to work for you:

Begin with an idea and a model of what your ideal client looks like. Who are they? What are they? What service do they need most? What price will they pay? What is the best kind of client you can have? Build a picture of what the best client looks like. When you have the ideal client firmly in mind, it's amazing how you're able to define what you're looking for and what you have.

The next thing is to **sort and qualify your database.** Who's in there? Who's on board? Who are the people most willing to refer you? Assemble your "A" list. Be selective. These are the people who will make the system work for you. Go deeper in your database, not wider. Color-code by type.

Put the people you're not sure of into "B" or "C" categories and store them in your database. Contact them in person over time. If your database is too large for that, send them a letter designed to spark a response and allow them to self-select. *"If you are interested in being part of my First Class Club, if you're interested in being on my Client Appreciation Program and receiving monthly Items of Value, please respond."*

If you have a small database, call each person and ask if they'd be interested in being part of your Client Appreciation Program. Are you somebody they'd refer in the future? And if they say no, you know what to do, delete. Don't be afraid if your client database shrinks radically. Size is not important. Quality is.

If you're just starting in business or rebuilding a list, a good source is community service organizations: Rotary, Kiwanis, Optimists, Lions Clubs, and Chamber of Commerce. So also are groups, associations, and social activities, friends and family members. For beginners, build your database in a burgeoning manner, then sort and qualify in stages. Make a list of everyone you know.

The object is to derive an "A+" list within a broader "A" list with the focus on quality. And with the realistic expectation that these people will refer you. It is extremely important to identify the "A+" clients. These people deserve and require your personal attention and involvement. The easiest and quickest way to generate new business is to go back to the people you've done business with in the past. They are already sold on you and happy to refer you. Go to them first.

And get rid of the clients you don't want. Say "bye-bye" nicely, like my son does when someone leaves our house. Don't be afraid to delete. It's necessary. Think of it as pruning a tree or weeding a garden.

After establishing your "A" list, **create a Client Appreciation Program** whereby you send Items of Value to these people on a consistent basis. If you've lost contact with some of the folks you've done business with in the past, send them a letter along with an Item of Value. Tell them: *"I really enjoyed serving you during our last transaction. But I must admit that I haven't stayed in as close contact as I would have liked. I recently made a commitment in my business to work exclusively by referral, and I'm going to send you Items of Value regularly. I'd like to get you back on board."* Then send them an Item of Value.

If you have a large database and a lot of people with whom you've stayed in contact, let them know that you will be raising your level of service to them. Introduce your Client Appreciation Program to them. You need to tell them this is a new day. *"You are one of my first class clients, and these Items of Value are my way of demonstrating my appreciation."* You want to let them know that. Educate your clients. Articulate how you work. Outline the benefits of working exclusively by referral.

The next thing is to **come up with the Items of Value that you send out every month.** Put them in two classifications: **Personal and Professional.** Personal communicates your character; Professional communicates your competence.

Remember, the Personal items don't need to relate to your business at all. They can be fun things or events: a get-together dinner, Super Bowl party, a game, a movie...as elaborate as a housewarming for a new home-buyer or as simple as a bag of popcorn. It should be something that you enjoy and think your clients will, too. The Professional items should connect somehow to your industry. People are always interested in ways to save money or inpertinent information on new homes. Be sure to make two lists...Personal and Professional...and send the items in balance to demonstrate character one time and competence the next time. Keep in mind that the main purpose of the items is to show people you're thinking of them and their needs. And follow up the Items of Value with a telephone call to each client sometime during the month.

The follow-up phone call sets up an appropriate opportunity for you to ask the person to reciprocate. The reciprocation you want is in the form of a referral. The best way to get that is to say: *"Oh, by the way, if you know someone who is thinking about buying or selling a home and would appreciate this same level of service, just give me a call with their name and number and I'd be happy to follow up with them for you."* Practice it until it's the most natural speech you've ever said. It's that important.

The most vital thing you can do is learn to ask for referrals. If you have staff, teach them how to ask for referrals. Make *"Oh, by the way..."* a part of your everyday lingo. Don't hang up the phone or end a conversation without saying it. If you're uncomfortable with how it sounds, call your own answering machine or voicemail and read the dialogue from a sheet of paper. Record yourself. You'll find that you sound pretty good. It's a nice surprise and a great way to practice. The only way you'll get really comfortable with it is by practicing. Eventually, the words will flow naturally from your mouth. You'll know you really have it when you're getting referrals and you don't remember asking for them. That's what this is all about. "Oh, by the way..." becomes your mantra. Make it part of your daily dialogue.

Client satisfaction comes through consideration manifested by communication with consistency.

To properly ask for a referral, use my Big 3 dialogue:

1. *"Can I be of any help to you or your business in any way? If I can, don't hesitate to call me."*
2. *"I want to make sure you know how much I value you as a client. I look forward to serving you."*
3. *"Oh, by the way..."*

Keep the client informed and current. The Items of Value followed by the personal telephone call in combination with the personal handwritten notes you send will constantly build more and more referrals. It will begin as a trickle and become a stream and then a flowing river.

Choose the number of personal notes and cards you will send out every day, and stick to it. In my real estate business, it was ten. Don't underestimate that; it's actually quite a lot. Ten every day. The key is to adhere to the daily discipline. I'd rather you sent five every day than ten once in awhile. Make sure you commit to a number you're comfortable with and will do every workday. Place the number of cards for the day by the phone you use. Turn it from a discipline into a habit. At the end of a phone conversation, pick up a pen and immediately write a personal note to that person. It will pay huge dividends.

The secret of success is constancy of purpose.
— Benjamin Disraeli

Don't forget to pop by on a regular basis and see your clients face to face. Nothing beats the personal contact. Bring an Item of Value for them, and follow up your visit by sending them a handwritten personal note. And don't forget to ask for a referral. "Oh, by the way..." should come at visit's end.

You've heard the old adage, "Jack of all trades, master of none." The key to anything is to learn how to master it. When you continually learn, do, and teach it, you will master it. Make the commitment to take at least one business owner to lunch each week. While you eat and chat, make it a point to teach them about the referral system.

Tell them how you are now doing business by referral. Teach them how to generate more referrals in their business. As you teach it to other people, you will learn it at a deeper level. Give it out in slices, it comes back in loaves; again my father's saying...appropriate for lunch. It's never so true as when you teach a better way to someone else. You'll find your dialogues improve. Your understanding of the process becomes that much stronger. Your ability to communicate it becomes a lot easier. Take a business owner to lunch each week, teach them the referral process, and at the end of the lunch, don't forget to say, *"Oh, by the way...".* What I found in my business experience is when I help people to grow their business, they can't do enough to help me grow mine.

In summary, study the elements of my system described in the first half of this book:

- ❑ Sort and qualify your database.
- ❑ Come up with Items of Value within your Client Appreciation Program.
- ❑ Learn to ask for referrals.

Know the components to use:

- ❑ Monthly Items of Value: Personal and Professional
- ❑ Calls to your database, ending with "Oh, by the way..."
- ❑ Pop-by visits to clients
- ❑ Taking business people to lunch to inform them about this system and ask for their referrals

Put all these elements together and use them consistently in proper sequence.

Most importantly, make the commitment to:

- ❑ Use the system wholeheartedly.
- ❑ Send ten notes every working day.
- ❑ Make 15 calls to your database every day.
- ❑ Send out at least one Item of Value every month.
- ❑ Take at least one business owner to lunch each week.
- ❑ Pop by at least 15 clients each week.

Make these your immediate goals, and you will have made a great start. You'll have the referral ball rolling. You'll be on your way to enjoying the benefits of doing business by referral with the clients you choose. Do it correctly with commitment, and they'll generate clients just like themselves. You'll do well, and you'll enjoy what you do. Selling exclusively by referral is a better way, all the way around.

Notice that I refer to my methods for generating referrals as a *system*. That's because it is, no matter how different or subjective it may appear to you. Don't be fooled into regarding it as collection of personal marketing or sales ploys because it does not live up to some preconceived notion. A system does not have to be computer-like or robotic, metallic and shiny. This is a human system, designed to be implemented and applied seriously within a program that requires strategy, commitment, and consistent application by people like you. That's what I designed it to do. It is engineered for psychological reaction and response and to meet interactive human needs. **Give. Ask. Receive.**

Each element and action I put forward in this system has been carefully considered, tested over time, and proved effective. And the system works to maximum efficiency when the elements are correctly combined, applied and sequenced with the proper motivation. Trust the system and work the system. Learn it, do it, teach it. Give this information out and you'll see it come back again and again. You're going to love what happens to your business and your life style, and you'll love teaching people to do the same. I do. Take it to heart.

The three major benefits of doing business by referral are:
More compatible people to work with. Clients trust you immediately because they trust the person who sent them to you.
More enthusiasm for your work. The better your relationship with clients, the more you will enjoy what you do; this in turn will make you more enthusiastic. It's a funny thing, the more enthusiastic you become, the more people will want to work with you.
More profitable business. It's a simple business equation in regard to profitability: when the cost of acquisition of a client is low, the profitability for that client is high.
Apply the referral system and principles, and these benefits will improve your business and your life. And that's my hope and prayer for each of you.

It's a good life! Am I right? Great! I hope to see you soon at one of our Turning Point Retreats. I'm looking forward to it. Thank you...and take care.

Oh, by the way, if you know of anyone who would appreciate this book and benefit from the information...

Acknowledgments

My first thanks go always to my coach and partner Beverly
for her love, support and good sense.

My great appreciation to Mort Keilty for his help
with all aspects of this book.

Thanks to my high school coach, Enda Carolyn,
my first mentor in business, Gene Kullman,
my brainstorming partner, Joe Niego,
the constant encouragement of Sam Elzie,
my brother Kevin, who has helped me through 800 seminars,
my brothers Gary, John and Dermot for their infinite support,

and the passionate people of Providence Systems,
who have taken a dream and made it a reality.

If you would like to get started or obtain more information on the referral system or coaching, please contact us at:

Providence Systems, Inc.
6349 Palomar Oaks Court
Carlsbad, CA 92009

phone: **(800) 945-3485**
website: **www.providencesystems.com**

To order, copy this page and send it in.

To order additional copies of the book:

Oh, by the way... is available at special quantity discounts for bulk purchases for sales promotions, premiums or educational use.

Special books or book excerpts also can be created to fit specific needs.

For details, write: **Providence Systems, Inc.,**

6349 Palomar Oaks Court, Carlsbad, CA 92009

ISBN 0-9715638-1-0 $19.95 u.s.

Payable in U.S. funds only. Postage & handling: U.S./Can. $5.00 for one book, $1.00 for each additional book. International: $8.00 for one book, $1.00 for each additional book. We accept Visa, MC, AMEX, Discover, checks ($15.00 fee for returned checks) and money orders. No cash/COD. Call 800-945-3485 or mail your orders to:

Providence Systems, Inc., 6349 Palomar Oaks Court, Carlsbad, CA 92009

Bill my credit card _____exp. _____

Visa _____ MC _____ AMEX _____ Discover_____

Signature_____

Bill to _____ Book Total $_____

Address _____

Applicable sales tax $ _____

City _____ST ____ZIP _____

Phone No. _____ Postage & handling $ _____

Ship to: _____

Address _____ Total amount due $ _____

City _____ST ____ZIP _____

Please allow 4-6 weeks for U.S. delivery. International orders allow 6-8 weeks.
This offer is subject to change without notice.